A NEW DIRECTION

A Cognitive-Behavioral Treatment Curriculum

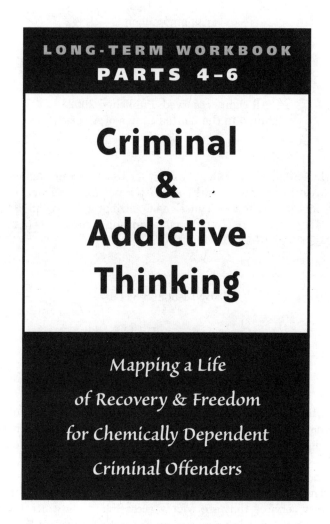

LONG-TERM WORKBOOK
PARTS 4–6

Criminal & Addictive Thinking

*Mapping a Life
of Recovery & Freedom
for Chemically Dependent
Criminal Offenders*

**A Collaboration of Chemical Dependency Professionals from
the Minnesota Department of Corrections and the Hazelden Foundation**

HAZELDEN®

Hazelden
Center City, Minnesota 55012-0176

1-800-328-9000
1-651-213-4590 (Fax)
www.hazelden.org

ISBN: 1-56838-841-1

Cover design by David Spohn
Interior design by Terri Kinne
Illustrations by Patrice Barton

Hazelden Publishing and Educational Services is a division of the Hazelden Foundation, a not-for-profit organization. Since 1949, Hazelden has been a leader in promoting the dignity and treatment of people afflicted with the disease of chemical dependency.

The mission of the foundation is to improve the quality of life for individuals, families, and communities by providing a national continuum of information, education, and recovery services that are widely accessible; to advance the field through research and training; and to improve our quality and effectiveness through continuous improvement and innovation.

Stemming from that, the mission of this division is to provide quality information and support to people wherever they may be in their personal journey—from education and early intervention, through treatment and recovery, to personal and spiritual growth.

The headquarters of the Hazelden Foundation are in Center City, Minnesota. Additional treatment facilities are located in Chicago, Illinois; New York, New York; Plymouth, Minnesota; St. Paul, Minnesota; and West Palm Beach, Florida. At these sites, we provide a continuum of care for men and women of all ages. Our Plymouth facility is designed specifically for youth and families.

For more information on Hazelden, please call **1-800-257-7800.** Or you may access our World Wide Web site on the Internet at **www.hazelden.org.**

CONTENTS

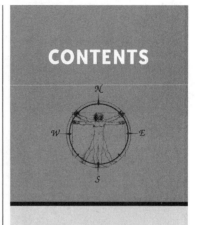

A NEW DIRECTION

A Cognitive-Behavioral Treatment Curriculum

Acknowledgments

The following people (whose titles and positions were current on the date of publication) have contributed to this curriculum:

Sheryl Ramstad Hvass
Commissioner, Minnesota Department of Corrections

Peter Bell
Executive Vice President, Hazelden Publishing and Educational Services

James D. Kaul, Ph.D.
Director, TRIAD Chemical Dependency Program
Minnesota Department of Corrections

Will Alexander
Sex Offender/Chemical Dependency Services Unit, Minnesota Department of Corrections

Minnesota Department of Corrections

Sex Offender Treatment Program at Lino Lakes Minnesota Correctional Facility

Robin Goldman, Director
Jim Berg, Program Supervisor
Brian Heinsohn, Corrections Program Therapist
Greg Kraft, Corrections Program Therapist
K. Kaprice Borowski Krebsbach, Corrections Program Therapist
Kevin Nelson, Corrections Program Therapist
Tim Schrupp, Corrections Program Therapist
Pamela Stanchfield, Corrections Program Therapist
Jason Terwey, Corrections Program Therapist
John Vieno, Corrections Program Therapist
Cynthia Woodward, Corrections Program Therapist

TRIAD Chemical Dependency Program at Lino Lakes Minnesota Correctional Facility

Launie Zaffke, Supervisor
Randy Tenge, Supervisor
Carmen Ihlenfeldt, Acting Supervisor
Thomas A. Berner, Corrections Program Therapist
Toni Brezina, Corrections Program Therapist
Jeanie Cooke, Corrections Program Therapist
Ronald J. DeGidio, Corrections Program Therapist
Susan DeGidio, Corrections Program Therapist
Maryann Edgerley, Corrections Program Therapist
Connie Garritsen, Corrections Program Therapist
Gerald Gibcke, Corrections Program Therapist
Anthony Hoheisel, Corrections Program Therapist
Deidra Jones, Corrections Program Therapist
Beth Matchey, Corrections Program Therapist
Jack McGee, Corrections Program Therapist
Jackie Michaelson, Corrections Program Therapist

Hal Palmer, Corrections Program Therapist
Terrance Peach, Corrections Program Therapist
Holly Petersen, Corrections Program Therapist
Linda Rose, Corrections Program Therapist
Kathy Thompson, Corrections Program Therapist
Beverly Welo, Corrections Program Therapist

Reshape Chemical Dependency Program at Saint Cloud Minnesota Correctional Facility

Robert L. Jungbauer, Director
Christine Fortson, Corrections Program Therapist
Tracanne Nelson, Corrections Program Therapist
Jeffrey D. Spies, Corrections Program Therapist

Atlantis Chemical Dependency Program at Stillwater Minnesota Correctional Facility

Bob Reed, Director
Dennis Abitz, Corrections Program Therapist
Bill Burgin, Corrections Program Therapist
Tom Shipp, Corrections Program Therapist

New Dimensions Chemical Dependency Program at Faribault Minnesota Correctional Facility

Michael Coleman, Supervisor
Michele Caron, Corrections Program Therapist

Central Office

Jim Linehan, Corrections Program Therapist

Minnesota Department of Corrections Supervising Agents

Russ Stricker, Correctional Unit Supervisor
Bobbi Chevaliar-Jones, Intensive Supervised Release Agent
William Hafner, Corrections Agent
Gregory Fletcher, 180 Degrees Halfway House

In Addition:

Writers: Corrine Casanova, Deborah Johnson, Stephen Lehman, Joseph M. Moriarity, Paul Schersten.
Designer: Terri Kinne. **Typesetters:** Terri Kinne, Julie Szamocki. **Illustrator:** Patrice Barton.
Prepress: Don Freeman, Kathryn Kjorlien, Rachelle Kuehl, Joan Seim, Tracy Snyder, David Spohn.
Editor: Corrine Casanova. **Copy editors:** Monica Dwyer Abress, Kristal Leebrick, Caryn Pernu.
Proofreaders: Catherine Broberg, Kristal Leebrick. **Training Consultant:** Derrick Crim.
Video production manager: Alexis Scott. **And special thanks to many others at Hazelden.**

Special thanks: Any Color Painting Company; Blue Moon Production Company; Eden Re-entry Services; inmates and staff of Lino Lakes, Rush City, and Stillwater Minnesota Correctional Facilities.

We are also indebted to Dr. Stanton E. Samenow, Ph.D., author of *Inside the Criminal Mind,* for his pioneering work on criminal thinking.

Getting Started on Workbook 2

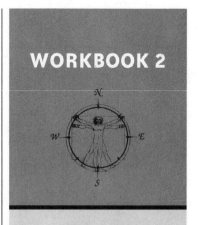

A NEW DIRECTION

A Cognitive-Behavioral Treatment Curriculum

Welcome to the second workbook of this Criminal and Addictive Thinking module. Here you will learn all about how criminal and addictive thinking patterns reinforce each other, how core beliefs lead to thinking and behavior, the progression of criminal development and recovery, the progression of addiction development and recovery, and criminal and addictive tactics. It's a lot of information to cover, but it's all essential for your recovery from a life of crime and abuse of alcohol and other drugs.

Before we get started, let's quickly review the Thinking Report, a tool you have been using to better understand your thinking and to develop new, healthy patterns of thinking.

A Thinking Report is a way for you to practice thinking about your thinking, your core beliefs, and your behavior so you change them. Thinking Reports are a very important tool in helping you learn how to read your inner map. Knowing how to think about your own thinking is the most important basic skill you need to create a new successful thought map.

The seven main parts of the Thinking Report are

1. The **Event**—what exactly happened to begin the chain of thoughts, feelings, and behaviors or potential behaviors.

2. Your **Thoughts**—what popped into your mind when the event occurred.

3. Your **Feelings**—the emotions or other sensations that resulted from your thoughts about the event.

4. Your **Behavior**—your actions in response to the event as directed by your thoughts and reinforced by your feelings.

5. Your **Core Beliefs**—the assumptions you make about the world, others, and yourself.

6. Possible **Alternative Thoughts**—healthier thoughts that are different from your first, automatic thoughts and that could lead to a more positive outcome.

7. Possible **Alternative Behaviors**—what you could do based on your alternative thoughts.

In Thinking Reports, you are also asked to identify any Thinking Distortions, Thinking Patterns, and Tactics you use.

- Thinking Distortions were discussed in part 3 of the first workbook. They are consistently inaccurate and biased ways that people use to look at themselves, others, and the world.

- Thinking Patterns, discussed in parts 3 and 4, are habits of thought. Criminal and Addictive Thinking Patterns are thinking problems that have led to behavior problems in your life.

- Tactics, discussed in part 6, are habits of behavior that result from your thinking patterns and core beliefs.

Now, turn back to page 63 of workbook 1 and write your answers from that Thinking Report here. We'll be referring to those answers later in this workbook. As you copy the sections from the Thinking Report that you've filled out so far, pay attention to any areas that may still be confusing for you and then discuss these in group or with your therapist. Remember, learning how to replace unsuccessful patterns of thinking with rational choices will, over time, create new patterns and lead you to a happier, healthier, more free way of life.

Thinking Report

1. Event _____

   _____

2. Thoughts _____

   _____

3. Feelings _____

   _____

4. Behavior _____

   _____

5. Can you identify a core belief? _____

   _____

6. Alternative thoughts _____

   _____

7. Alternative behavior _____

   _____

Thinking distortions _____

Thinking patterns _____

Tactics _____

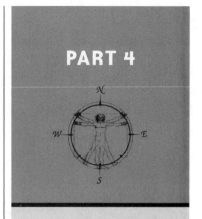

PART 4

**A NEW
DIRECTION**

*A Cognitive-Behavioral
Treatment Curriculum*

Learning to Think about Your Thinking

ADDICTIVE THINKING PATTERNS AND CORE BELIEFS

As an addict, you have unhealthy thinking patterns that take you back to using time and again. As you continue to better understand how and why you think the way you do, you can begin to make the kinds of changes that will lead you to recovery.

Addictive Thinking Patterns

Addictive thinking patterns are very similar to criminal thinking patterns. In most cases, the only differences are in degree or in the particular direction the thinking takes. Remember the definition of criminal thinking patterns? *Criminal thinking patterns* are ways of thinking that say it is okay to violate others or the property of others.

The definition of addictive thinking patterns is similar: *Addictive thinking patterns* are ways of thinking that say it is okay to use as much drugs and alcohol as you want, as often as you want, and to do whatever you need to do to get them.

Thoughts that suggest, justify, or promote getting drunk and high no matter what the consequences to you or to others will most likely fit into one or more of the addictive thinking patterns categories.

Here are the addictive thinking patterns we've identified:

- self-pity stance
- "good person" stance
- "unique person" stance
- fear of exposure
- lack-of-time perspective
- selective effort
- use of deceit to control
- seek pleasure first
- ownership stance

*Addiction is a **thinking** problem before it becomes a **drinking** problem.*

Denial

The main feature of addictive thinking is **denial.** Denial for the addict and alcoholic refers to the ability to contradict obvious facts, to turn the truth inside out, to look directly at *down* and to believe, with all your heart and mind, that it is really *up*.

One of the interesting features of denial is that you can often see in others what you can't see in yourself. Therefore, you may say something like, "Poor Pete. What a fool. He keeps drinking until he passes out, gets beat up, and rolled. What a chump." You can clearly see how pathetic Pete's situation is. What you can't see is how pathetic your own situation can be. You can't see how your alcohol or other drug use has gotten you in so much trouble that you've lost just about everything. Now you're incarcerated, probably not for the first time.

You haven't been able to see the truth about your own alcohol or other drug use because of your denial. To see that truth would mean you'd have to try recovery. It would mean you'd have to stop using. And that is what your addictive thinking calls you to deny—anything that would suggest you need to stop using.

> **Denial**
>
> *Denial* is used by addicts and alcoholics to keep themselves unaware of the harmful consequences of their use. Though addicts and alcoholics often lie to get what they want, denial is not about lying to others. Denial is a trick the addict's mind plays on itself to excuse the use of alcohol or other drugs no matter what harm it does.

Self-Obsession

As an addict, you are pleasure-centered and self-centered. That means your thoughts focus on whether or not you feel good. If you don't feel good, you become preoccupied with what you can do to make yourself feel good again as soon as possible. You had a powerful pleasure experience with drugs or alcohol (or with sex or gambling or eating or anything else people get addicted to) when you first used, and your mind became obsessed with repeating that

Denial is not a river in Egypt.

experience. When you feel bad, all you can think about is how to get drugs (alcohol, sex, and so on) so you will feel like you felt that first time you experienced them.

Because you are obsessed with feeling good, you tend to think only about your own wants and needs. Only after your wants and needs are met (for the moment, at least) are you able to consider the wants and needs of others.

Irrational Thinking

Because your thinking is driven by the obsession to feel good, it becomes *irrational*. Irrational thoughts lead to out-of-whack emotions and irrational behavior.

As an addict, you often use irrational thinking because you are not looking to find the truth. You are only looking to justify and excuse your single-minded search for the high. That is why your logic usually goes around in circles, even when it may seem to make sense on the surface.

Irrational Thinking

Irrational thinking is thinking that is inconsistent with the facts. It contradicts itself and is confused, disorderly, and distorted. Irrational thinking does not use reason to find the truth; it makes arguments to try to prove a lie.

The Addict's Logic

A man is sitting at a bar. He is drunk. It is the tenth day in a row he has gone into the bar, sat on the same stool, and drunk until he nearly passed out.

"Why do you drink so much?" the bartender finally asks him.

"I drink because my wife doesn't understand me," replies the drunk.

"What doesn't she understand?" asks the bartender.

"She doesn't understand why I drink so much," says the man.

Why Do You Use?

➤ So why *do* you drink or use drugs? List five of your reasons—your excuses and rationalizations—for getting high. List the things you tell yourself and the things you tell others. Start each sentence with "I use drugs because . . ." or "I drink alcohol because . . ." Leave line 6 blank.

1. _____

2. _____

3. _____

4. _____

5. _____

6. _____

Now that you have listed the top five reasons you *think* you use alcohol or other drugs, here's the real reason:

You use alcohol or other drugs because you're a drug addict or an alcoholic.

➤ Now go back to your list of reasons for using and write the real reason on line 6: *I use drugs [or alcohol] because I'm a drug addict [or an alcoholic].*

Rational or Irrational Thinking?

Again, irrational thinking is confused or distorted thinking that contradicts the hard facts. Identify the following thoughts as either rational or irrational.

➤ Circle **R** for *rational* and **I** for *irrational.*

R   I   "Insurance pays for stuff that gets ripped off, so nobody really gets hurt."

R   I   "I'm really disappointed when I make a mistake and people get down on me."

R   I   "These homework assignments are really a pain to do."

R   I   "My therapist is always singling me out. She hates me and is out to make my time miserable."

R   I   "The therapists and administrators get paid a bonus for every one of us that gets kicked out of treatment."

R   I   "It's really a shame things didn't work out better than they did."

R   I   "I can't believe I relapsed. Face it—I'm just a loser."

R   I   "I'm better than just about everybody in so many ways."

R   I   "Damn! I wanted to play some hoops. I wish it wasn't raining."

R   I   "Flunking that class was a huge disappointment."

R   I   "They left it lying out in their yard. I found it. Now it's mine."

R   I   "I won't get caught next time because I won't make the same mistake I made before."

R   I   "Most women like forced sex."

R   I   "Some people have it easier in life than other people."

R   I   "Just because others get messed up by drugs doesn't mean I can't handle it. I'm tougher than they are."

R   I   "Listening to that music is really annoying."

R   I   "I wish I could have had the visit today."

R   I   "The therapists in this program love it when we fail."

R   I   "Trying to change my thinking is a lot of work."

R   I   "I've ruined everything I've touched in my life."

R   I   "If she didn't like getting hit, she wouldn't have come back home."

R   I   "Life isn't always fair."

Self-Pity Stance

As an addict, you have your own version of the victim-stance criminal thinking pattern. It's called the **self-pity stance.** You think the world is out to get you, that you're just a victim of bad luck. You have a hard time taking responsibility for what happens to you. You see yourself as the victim. In fact, if you're really pushed, you'd likely accept any explanation for how miserable and screwed up your life can be—as long as that explanation doesn't point a finger at your drug or alcohol use.

That *is* insane thinking. But it's not the result of mental illness—it's the result of your addiction to alcohol or other drugs.

"Poor me. Poor me. Poor me. Pour me . . . a drink."

—Recovery saying

EXERCISE 57 EXERCISE

Identifying Self-Pity Thinking

Self-pity thinking is one important way you justify your use of alcohol or other drugs. The following thoughts are examples of the self-pity stance:

- "I grew up in a tough neighborhood. I had to fight for survival. Having a hit or two now and then is the least I deserve for all I went through."

- "My dad was a drunk and my mom shot heroin. It's not my fault I use."

- "When I was in school, I always got punished for stuff I didn't do. Life's always been unfair to me."

➤ List three self-pitying thoughts you had last week.

1. _____

2. _____

3. _____

➤ Explain how your self-pity stance has set you up to use in the past.

_____

_____

_____

Despite all the things you've messed up, you still think you're a decent person.

"Good Person" Stance

Despite all the things you've messed up and all the times you've let yourself and other people down, you still think you're a decent person. As an addictive thinker, you use four main strategies to create and maintain the illusion that you are essentially a good person, no matter what. They are the same strategies you use as a criminal thinker, only you also use them to justify your chemical use. These strategies are

- sentimentality
- selective memory
- excuses and rationalizations
- false comparisons and self-serving definitions

You use these strategies to avoid thinking about yourself realistically. If you saw yourself clearly and realistically, it would be obvious even to you how drugs or alcohol have messed up your life and led you to hurt yourself and others. The purpose of "good person" stance thinking, like all other addictive thinking patterns, is to justify your continued use.

Sentimentality

Sentimentality is viewing your motives and intentions as always "good" on some level.

As an addictive thinker using the "good person" stance, you focus on the good things you've done and ignore the harm. You get ***sentimental*** about your mother but forget the times you lied to her or stole from her. Or you talk about how much your kids mean to you, even though you can't remember their birthdays. Or you try to make yourself look good by continually pointing out that someone else is worse than you. You say, "At least I'm not a crack head," or "I'm no gutter drunk like that guy." You believe in an addictive hierarchy just like you believe in a criminal hierarchy. The idea that some drugs are somehow "better" than other drugs, however, is delusional. They all do the same thing to your brain in the end—they hijack it. And they'll all kill you, sooner or later.

EXERCISE **58** EXERCISE

Can "Good" People Use Alcohol or Other Drugs?

➤ How does your view of yourself as a good person help you justify your use of alcohol or other drugs?

_____

_____

_____

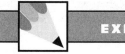

Your Hierarchy of Drug Use

➤ List your hierarchy of drugs in order, from the "best" to the worst/most degrading. (Remember, alcohol *is* a drug.)

1. _____

2. _____

3. _____

4. _____

5. _____

6. _____

➤ What makes drugs 1 and 2 better drugs to use?

_____

_____

_____

_____

➤ What makes drugs 5 and 6 worse drugs to use?

_____

_____

_____

_____

➤ How do you use your hierarchy of drugs to justify your own chemical use?

_____

_____

_____

_____

■

"Unique Person" Stance

As an addictive thinker, you like to see yourself as different and special. You also tend to romanticize yourself. You may see yourself as a mysterious, adventurous, or tragic figure, like a pirate or an old-west cowboy or a gangster or some other super-bad, super-tough character.

You also think you are always right and have great difficulty admitting your mistakes. You are self-righteous. That means you will do whatever it takes to prove you are right—shouting down others, arguing over every little thing, bullying others into agreement or silence.

You use the **"unique person" stance** to feed your addiction. Perhaps you think your drug or alcohol use makes you especially cool—the hard drinker/smoker/snorter who can use more than anyone else and still be standing at the end of the night.

Your addiction is really the least unique thing about you. The truth is, you have a very common disease that has clear symptoms, familiar thought and behavior patterns, and predictable results. The story of your addiction is more or less the same as every other addict's story.

Here are examples of addictive thinking using the "unique person" stance:

- "I can drink anybody under the table."

- "Crack takes me places you can't even dream of."

- "I've smuggled more junk without getting caught than you'll ever see in your lifetime."

- "Don't tell me about what drugs do. I've forgotten more about chemicals than you'll ever know."

EXERCISE 60 EXERCISE

Your So-Called Unique Addiction

➤ List three things you have told yourself that were different about your alcohol or other drug use than anybody else's.

1. _____

_____

2. _____

_____

3. _____

_____

Fear of Exposure

Just as your criminal thinking patterns are filled with many fears, so are your addictive thinking patterns. Here are four features of addictive **fear of exposure:**

- fear of self-knowledge
- excessive or inappropriate trust
- addict pride
- zero state

The first three represent a fear of change. You fear you'll be exposed as an addict or alcoholic and will have to stop using. So you hide your use or you flaunt it. You hide it so others won't know about your use and challenge it, or you flaunt it as a power move to make it seem like nothing can hurt you. Either way, you are afraid to take a good, hard look at your chemical use because you are afraid of changing your life in ways that might mean changing your use.

The zero state represents a fear that you cannot change, that you will get trapped in an intolerable condition of emptiness. In the zero state, you are frantic to change—though the *only* thing you really want to change is how bad you feel.

Fear of Self-Knowledge

You are afraid that if you really found out who you are, deep down, you might see that you are nothing. This is fear of the zero state that we discussed in criminal thinking patterns. You avoid self-knowledge to avoid looking at this fear—the fear that you might be worthless.

As an addict, you base trust on who might help you get high and who won't.

Excessive or Inappropriate Trust

As an addict, you base trust on who might help you get high and who won't. You tend to trust untrustworthy people who promise to help you get high. You tend to distrust trustworthy people who discourage or try to block your chemical use. Your trust is not based on facts or logic or even your own good sense of who is honest and who isn't.

Addict Pride

Most addicts have a sense of pride about their drug of choice. They think it is somehow better than other drugs. So a crack smoker might think heroin addicts are degraded for injecting their drug, while heroin addicts might say crack users are sick for how they can desperately chase the high for days on end in the worst conditions. Alcoholics may think their drug is better because it's legal, while ecstasy users think theirs is the coolest drug.

Zero State

As an addict, you also go into the zero state from time to time—the belief that you are worthless, nobody, empty inside. While your criminal thinking tends to use power over others as a way to escape the zero state, your addictive thinking tends to use deceit to control others or increased chemical use to find relief. In both cases, however, you will use both deceit and power to escape zero state, and you'll often use them together. As an addict *and* a criminal, you will use any of those strategies—whatever seems to work at the time.

As an addict, you tend to look on the dark side of things. You expect the worst and often see the worst in situations and others. Just as you use your expectation of an early death to justify your criminal behavior, you use the same dark thinking as an excuse to get high. You think, "If I'm doomed anyway, why not?"

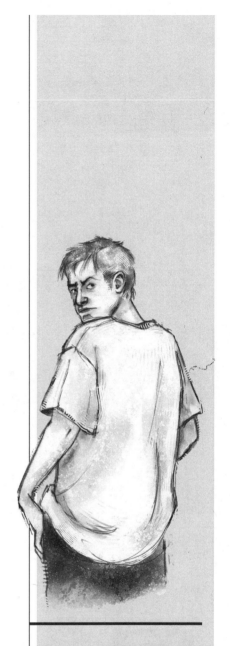

You look on the dark side of things. You expect the worst and see the worst in situations and others.

Despite your thoughts of impending doom, when it comes to your chemical use, you also have an irrational belief that alcohol and other drugs will not have a harmful effect on your body and brain. You assume they won't have the same destructive results on your body that they have on everyone else's.

So either you *deny* the harm of chemical use or you *accept* it because you don't care, since you're doomed anyway.

Remember the continuum of fear you looked at in the section on criminal thinking patterns? It looks like this:

Figure 15
THE CONTINUUM OF FEAR

Too Afraid	Healthy Fear	No Fear
Has so many fears, many of them irrational, that he can't make a healthy decision.	Has rational fears that guide him to take care of himself and motivate him to make healthy decisions for change	Lacks rational fears—thinks he's infallible and invulnerable—and doesn't think he needs to make any changes. Thinks he's invincible (cannot be defeated or caught) and invisible at the same time.

As an addict, you tend to live on both extremes of this continuum: either full of irrational fears or lacking the healthy fears that might protect you. One of the reasons you may be "too afraid" is that many mind-altering chemicals tend to cause ***paranoia*** in the user. Meth, angel dust, and marijuana are some of the drugs whose users have reported experiencing paranoia.

Paranoia

Paranoia is a mental condition of extreme suspiciousness and lack of trust. When you are paranoid, you have an irrational belief that people are out to get you. You may think everyone is looking at you, talking about you behind your back, or plotting against you even though it is not true.

You also lack healthy fears that would keep you from harm, especially in regard to your chemical use. That is why you are willing to put some pill or powder you bought from a dealer you may not even know into your body. Because getting high is more important to you than your own physical safety, you are willing to believe exactly what the dealer tells you. You trust this even when you know the dealer to be a highly untrustworthy person! You trust this even when you know the drug has been cut, and you know what you have used to cut stuff yourself.

EXERCISE **61** EXERCISE

Risk Taking

➤ Give three examples of serious risks you have taken to get high.

1. _____

2. _____

3. _____

➤ Is there anything else in your life (besides chemicals) that is so attractive it would lead you to take such risks? If so, what is it?

_____

_____

_____

Lack-of-Time Perspective

Because getting high (feeling intense pleasure) is the most important thing in your life, you tend to live only in the present when you are high and only in the near future ("How can I get more soon?") when you are not high. This **lack-of-time perspective** is one feature of your thinking that denies the health damage and social consequences of using by blocking out thoughts of the long-term future.

Your lack-of-time perspective also shows up in how you get cause and effect mixed up. *Cause and effect* means that when you do A (cause), then B (effect) happens. For example, if you jump in a lake (cause), you will get wet (effect).

It seems pretty simple. But what about the following causes and effects?

- If you steal your girlfriend's money to buy drugs (cause), she will get angry and upset and nag you about your irresponsibility (effect).

- If you get drunk all the time (cause), you will lose your job (effect).

In the addict's deluded (reversed) version of cause and effect, the thinking goes like this:

- Because my girlfriend nags and gets angry all the time (cause), I get high (effect).

- Because they fire me from every job (cause), I drink (effect).

By reversing cause and effect in the moment, you fail to look at what happened in the past—that your chemical use created serious problems. You also can't see what will happen in the future—that more serious problems will be caused by continued use of alcohol and other drugs if you don't stop now. Your chemical use is not the *result* of your problems; it is the primary *cause* of them—past, present, and future.

Thinking about the Past and Future

➤ List three examples of when your use of alcohol or other drugs (cause) has led to negative consequences (effect).

1. _____

   _____

2. _____

   _____

3. _____

   _____

➤ Imagine your life five years from now if you were to continue using alcohol or other drugs. What will it be like? What will *you* be like?

_____

_____

_____

_____

Selective Effort

As an addictive thinker, you will go to great trouble to get and use alcohol and other drugs. Just as you have plenty of energy when you need it for crime, you can go without food and sleep in your pursuit of getting high. However, when it comes to the day-to-day obligations of responsible living, you can't be bothered. You're too tired or too un-interested—or too busy getting high.

In part, this is because of your unwillingness to tolerate frustration. You often won't make the effort to try anything new or difficult because

1. If you fail, it might send you into the zero state.

2. You are afraid of all change, because growth and change threaten your using.

Your **selective effort** is part of the self-centeredness of your addictive thinking. You have the energy to fulfill your own pleasure desires, but not enough for others, including your children or other loved ones. You have the drive to score and use chemicals, but not to find and keep a job or finish school.

Codependence

Codependence is abandoning yourself— your own needs and growth and develop- ment opportunities—in order to give all your energies to taking care of someone else. Codependence is an unhealthy way of thinking and living.

Magical Thinking and Codependency
Selective effort is more than self-centered-ness. It is also a feature of your magical thinking. You tend to think that somehow things will work out without you having to make any effort. You think that somehow the trouble you've gotten yourself into will just go away. This magical thinking probably followed you into treatment.

It is also often the result of the **codependent** thinking of others. Since you are generally unwilling to make an effort, you try to get other people to make the effort for you. You want them to clean up all the messes you create with your chemical abuse, to do the work (effort) that is your responsibility, and to take care of you.

It is not surprising that addicts and alcoholics seek out codependents and that codependents seek out addicts and alcoholics. It is a powerful attraction. It is also an unhealthy relationship because each helps the other continue the thinking and behavior that is most destructive for them. Over time, codependents and addicts/alcoholics will (1) make themselves and each other miserable, and (2) eventually destroy their own and each other's lives.

EXERCISE **63** EXERCISE

Identifying Your Selective Efforts

➤ What obligations and responsibilities have you blown off to use chemicals?

_____

_____

_____

_____

_____

_____

Naming Your Codependents

➤ List the codependents in your life by asking the following questions: Who sends you money? Who raises your kids? Who do you expect to take care of your business, the obligations and responsibilities you listed in exercise 63?

1. Name _____

What do you expect of this person?

_____

2. Name _____

What do you expect of this person?

_____

3. Name _____

What do you expect of this person?

_____

4. Name _____

What do you expect of this person?

_____

Use of Deceit to Control

Both criminal and addictive thinkers believe they need to control others and situations. Addictive thinking says it is okay to use chemicals. When people challenge you on this, you want to control them. You believe that if you can control others and situations, you can continue with your chemical abuse.

As a criminal, you try to control others mainly through power tactics. As an addict, you try to control others mainly through lies. Since you are both a criminal and an addict, you use a mixture of both power and deceit, with each feeding into the other.

Using deceit to control means you will lie, cheat, steal, tell half-truths, and beg to get and continue using alcohol or other drugs. Denial is one form of deception. It is deceiving yourself about the harm of your chemical use. As an addict, however, you are also willing to lie to others as much as necessary in order to keep using. This kind of lying is different from denial—it is aggressive, self-centered, and extremely damaging to all your relationships.

The addictive thinking that uses deceit to control takes three directions:

1. You tend to become defensive when challenged about your chemical use, or you tell half-truths or make empty promises about quitting.

2. You must always be right about everything, since being wrong threatens your illusion of control. Therefore, you argue frequently and exaggerate to "win" arguments.

3. You will use this controlling power of deceit to keep others off balance to avoid challenges to your chemical use and maintain your source of supply.

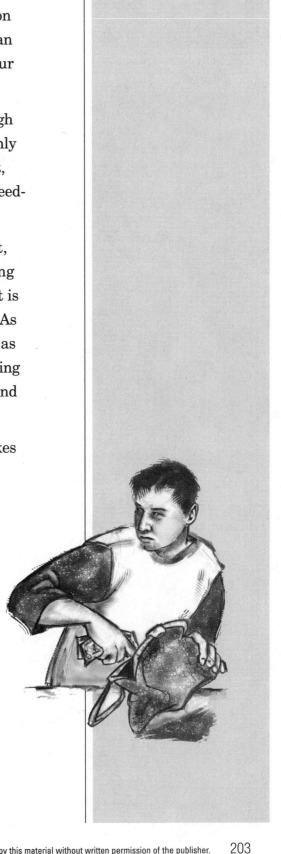

Who Have You Lied To?

As an addict, you will lie to anyone who might stand in the way of your getting or using alcohol or other drugs. Usually, these are the people closest to you: your spouse or significant other, kids, parents or grandparents, friends, neighbors, co-workers, and employers.

► Name five people you have lied to in order to get, use, or get away with using alcohol or other drugs. Then describe how the lies were designed to control that person's behavior so you could keep using.

Person you
lied to

How did the lies you told
control that person?

1. _____   _____

_____

2. _____   _____

_____

3. _____   _____

_____

4. _____   _____

_____

5. _____   _____

_____

EXERCISE **66** EXERCISE

The People Closest to You

➤ List the three most important people in your life. Then list three lies you told each of them in order to get, use, or get away with using alcohol or other drugs.

Name of person close to you: _____

Lies you told this person in order to use:

    1. _____

    2. _____

    3. _____

Name of person close to you: _____

Lies you told this person in order to use:

    1. _____

    2. _____

    3. _____

Name of person close to you: _____

Lies you told this person in order to use:

    1. _____

    2. _____

    3. _____

➤ How did your lies give you control (even for a short time) over these people?

_____

_____

_____

➤ How did these and other lies affect your relationships with these people?

_____

_____

_____

➤ What does it mean to you that you are willing to lie to the people who are most important in your life so you can get high?

_____

_____

_____

Seek Pleasure First

As a criminal thinker, you tend to seek excitement first and worry about consequences later (if at all). This impulsiveness is also a part of your addictive thinking. As an addictive thinker, you tend to **seek pleasure first**—the pleasure of getting high. You will seek this pleasure without regard for the serious physical, mental, and legal consequences that result. Even after your body begins to build a tolerance to your drug(s) of choice and it becomes more and more difficult to find a good high, you continue to seek, out of habit and physical craving, the drug-induced pleasure you once felt.

Addiction is a powerful mental and physical habit, driven by your memories of pleasurable drug experiences, your body's craving for the drug, and your unwillingness to tolerate discomfort. That means that when you feel frustrated, bored, anxious, or uncomfortable, your first thought is to relieve that discomfort

> **Obsession**
>
> An *obsession* is a powerful and persistent idea or feeling that demands almost all your attention.

as quickly as possible, and the fastest way you know to do that is with chemicals. Once you get the idea that you need to get high, little can stand in your way. You'll generally do whatever you need to do to find and use alcohol or other drugs. This is called *obsession,* and "seek pleasure first" thinking is the way your mind feeds your obsession with getting high.

One of the problems with your use of alcohol or other drugs and the thinking that leads you to seek pleasure first is that you identify happiness or feeling stress-free with being high.

A drug or alcohol high is a very temporary state.

Your body can't stand being intoxicated for long without breaking down. So when you are between highs or when your body develops **tolerance** and the high is less intense, it becomes very difficult for you to feel good. In this way, your "seek pleasure first" thinking actually leads you to more and more misery over time—and less and less pleasure. You become increasingly dissatisfied with everything and everybody, and you may find that even things that used to bring you joy no longer do.

Tolerance

Tolerance is the body's increasing resistance to the effects of a drug that results from frequent use over time.

EXERCISE 67 EXERCISE

Seeking Pleasure First

➤ List the main ways that you seek pleasure first when you are feeling bad or stressed. Be sure to list the behaviors, including chemical use (listing the specific drugs you'd choose), that you use to try to cover up uncomfortable feelings.

1. _____

2. _____

3. _____

4. _____

5. _____

6. _____

Dealing with Discomfort

Discomfort is a temporary state. When you feel bad, it can seem as if you will feel this way forever. This is not true: Comfort and discomfort come and go in life all the time. Nobody can feel good all the time, and the bad feelings also will pass with time (except with certain illnesses, of course).

➤ When you feel uncomfortable, your mind turns to ways of feeling better immediately rather than working through the discomfort. List two situations that make you feel anxious, uneasy, angry, irritated, or uncomfortable in some way.

1. _____

2. _____

➤ When you are in such situations, what are the first three things you think of doing to make yourself feel better?

1. _____

2. _____

3. _____

➤ What if you didn't do anything to make yourself feel better in such situations? What could you do to work through your discomfort instead of trying to cover it up?

_____

_____

Ownership Stance

When you learned about criminal thinking, the **ownership stance** was summed up in two ideas:

- one-way property boundaries
  ("What's mine is mine, and what's yours is mine.")

- the idea that people are property
  ("She's mine, so she has to do as I say.")

With addictive thinking, this ownership stance and its disregard for the property rights of others comes from your obsession with getting high. Since you will do whatever it takes to feed your addiction, you mistakenly believe it is somehow okay for you to steal and to cheat others to get what you want most: drugs or alcohol. You also often treat others as if their purpose in life is to help you feel better—to get you drugs or alcohol, or provide you with sex, and to clean up the messes you make. This thinking turns people into property for you. It defeats the possibility of having a healthy relationship.

One of the ways you treat others as property is by expecting them to constantly behave in ways to better meet your needs. You have been unwilling, however, to make changes in yourself. You have decided somewhere along the road that the world should adjust to you rather than you adjusting to the world. That kind of ownership-stance thinking says the world is yours to use and violate in any way you wish to get what you want.

It's not hard to understand why people with this kind of thinking end up behind bars! Ownership-stance thinking separates you from others because you don't care about anyone else's real needs or rights. So you see, long before you were separated from society by being locking up, you had already separated yourself out from family, friends, and community with your ownership-stance thinking.

You have been unwilling to make changes in yourself.

The Property of Others

➤ List five things you stole to get drugs or alcohol.

1. _____

2. _____

3. _____

4. _____

5. _____

➤ Describe some of the thoughts you had to justify stealing these things.

1. _____

2. _____

3. _____

➤ Why do you think it's okay for you to take the property of others but not okay for others to take your property?

_____

_____

_____

People Are Not Property

➤ Who are the people you used to help you get and use alcohol or other drugs? List three of them (by first name or initials only, if you choose). These are people you expect to provide excuses or to cover up for you. They are also friends, relatives, or acquaintances you have stolen from or ripped off in other ways (including dealers you bought drugs from and people you sold drugs to), and strangers you have cheated or robbed to buy drugs. (You may identify the strangers in any way that makes sense to you. For example, you could write, "The owner of the blue Buick" if, for example, you had stolen a CD player from a blue Buick in order to get money for drugs.)

People you used   How you used them

1. _____   _____

                                     _____

                                     _____

2. _____   _____

                                     _____

                                     _____

3. _____   _____

                                     _____

                                     _____

➤ What would you have to do to live in a way that did not use others as if they were your property?

_____

_____

_____

_____

Changing Addictive Thinking

To review, addictive thinking patterns are ways of thinking that say it is okay to use drugs and alcohol whenever you want to and as much as you want to. These thinking patterns also give you the go-ahead to do whatever you need to do to get drugs and alcohol. The patterns justify getting drunk and high no matter what the consequences to yourself or to others.

Here are the main addictive thinking patterns:

- self-pity stance
- "good person" stance
- "unique person" stance
- fear of exposure
- lack-of-time perspective
- selective effort
- use of deceit to control
- seek pleasure first
- ownership stance

Denial is the most important feature of addictive thinking. Denial is the way addicts and alcoholics keep themselves unaware of the terrible consequences of their use.

To change your addictive thinking patterns, you first need to learn to recognize the patterns as the thoughts happen. Second, you need to slow down, stop the rush to always feel good, and think for a moment. Because you liked the intensity of the high and how it made you feel, you tend to focus on the immediate pleasure but not the long-term pain.

This is the big lie that you have been telling yourself: that drugs bring you pleasure but have no consequences. The truth is, they probably played a big role in why you are locked up right now or have been locked up in the past.

EXERCISE **71** EXERCISE

Becoming Aware of Your Addictive Thinking

Think back to the last time you really wanted to get high. It might have been last week, yesterday, or an hour ago. If necessary, complete this exercise in a notebook.

➤ What was the situation? Where were you and who were you with? What was being talked about? What did you hear, smell, see, or taste that you associated with getting high?

_____

_____

_____

_____

➤ What did you feel in your body at the time? The physical symptoms of cravings vary with different people, so you need to learn what *your* symptoms are. For example, your stomach may have tightened up or you may have gotten the sweats. Perhaps your heart beat faster or you felt fatigued. Maybe your mouth began to water or got very dry. Describe exactly how you were feeling.

_____

_____

_____

➤ What was your emotional state? Again, it can be different for different people. You may have felt agitated or calm, sad, angry, frustrated, joyful, panicked, or bored. You may have felt many different things all at once. List them all.

_____

_____

➤ What were you thinking at the time? This may be the hardest to remember, but it's also the most important. You may have started thinking about drinking or about how to score something and then use it. Perhaps you tried to convince yourself to resist the urge. Be very specific in describing your thoughts.

_____

_____

_____

Here are the main
addictive thinking patterns:

- self-pity stance
- "good person" stance
- "unique person" stance
- fear of exposure
- lack-of-time perspective
- selective effort
- use of deceit to control
- seek pleasure first
- ownership stance

➤ List the addictive thinking patterns that you use the most.

1. _____

2. _____

3. _____

4. _____

Relapse Indicators

The thoughts and feelings you listed in exercise 71 can trigger cravings and cause relapse. (They will be discussed at much greater length in the Relapse Prevention module of this treatment program.) Think of them as danger signs along the roadway, such as "Bridge Out," "Beware Falling Rocks," or the flashing red lights of fire engines and ambulances. When you become aware of these relapse indicators, you need to, in a sense, slow down and pull over to the side of the road. You need to think hard about who you are and where you want to go before proceeding on in the same direction you're headed. When the signs say "Danger Ahead," there's danger ahead. When your relapse indicators come up, relapse isn't far away.

How Criminal and Addictive Thinking Patterns Reinforce Each Other

Criminal and addictive thinking patterns are not only similar, they also feed each other. Criminal thinking patterns will lead you to addictive thinking patterns and vice versa. This means that if you commit a crime, the thinking involved will likely lead you to use alcohol or other drugs. If you use drugs or alcohol, the thinking that convinces you to do that will quite possibly lead you back to criminal activity. You begin to think you are invincible and invisible again—nothing can stop you and you won't get caught because you're too careful and slick. (See figure 16 on page 218.)

Drugs and alcohol lower your inhibitions and increase your impulsivity. Inhibitions are thought patterns that hold you in check and prevent you from doing something. A value system that says it's wrong to steal is an inhibition against stealing. The ability to understand another person's pain is an inhibition against hurting others. A belief that drugs or alcohol and criminal behavior are ruining your life and hurting your loved ones can be an inhibition against relapse and committing crimes in the future.

You are short on healthy inhibitions to begin with.

But when you lower them by getting drunk or high, you become even more impulsive and self-destructive. The following exercises will help you see how your addiction and your criminality work together to mess up your life.

Figure 16
HOW CRIMINAL AND ADDICTIVE THINKING DRIVE EACH OTHER

ADDICTIVE THINKING

Controls with Deceit
  manipulates with lies
  undermines & confuses
  passive-aggressive
  abusive
  cheats and cons

Self-Obsessed
  self is shameful
  self-pitying
  loner
  unique
  resentful

Irresponsible
  false promises
  sexually selfish
  impulsive
  unreliable
  denies facts
  ducks obligations

False Pride
  self is special
  grandiose
  sentimental
  cynical
  fear of death
  self is smarter
  intolerant

Pleasure Focused
  craves sensuality
  instant gratification
  lustful
  low discomfort tolerance

Rigid
  self-righteous
  defensive
  need to be right
  perfectionistic
  judgmental
  absolutist

CRIMINAL THINKING

Controls with Power
  manipulates with threats
  undermines & confuses
  intimidates
  abusive
  cheats and cons

Self-Centered
  self is nothing (zero)
  self is victim
  loner
  unique
  entitled

Irresponsible
  lack of effort
  sexually predatory
  impulsive
  unreliable
  distorts facts
  refuses obligations

Criminal Pride
  self is good person
  extremely high self-image
  sentimental
  cynical
  fear of humiliation
  self is tougher
  quick temper

Excitement Focused
  craves thrills
  instant gratification
  power hungry
  low boredom tolerance

Concrete
  self-righteous
  close-minded
  need to be on top
  perfectionistic
  all or nothing
  absolutist

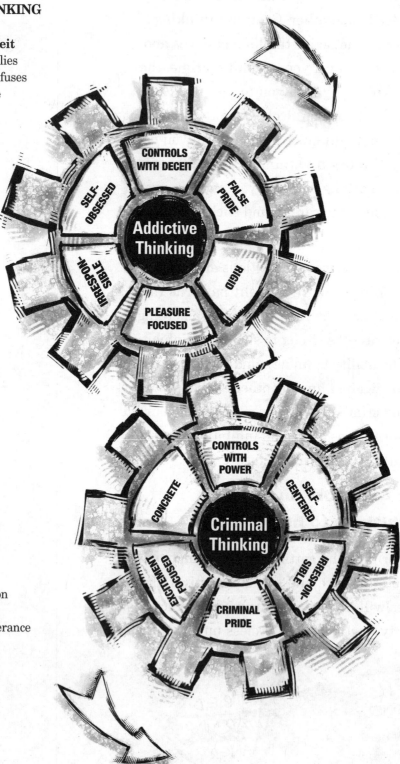

Your Drug and Alcohol Crimes

➤ List some crimes you committed to get drunk or high.

_____

_____

_____

➤ List crimes you committed *while* you were drunk or high.

_____

_____

_____

➤ Are there crimes you believe you might *not* have committed if it weren't for your alcohol or drug use? List them.

_____

_____

_____

If you have not already done so, you are now ready to start identifying the addictive thinking patterns and alternative thoughts and adding them to your Thinking Report on page 179.

Core Beliefs

Remember, core beliefs are those generalized beliefs or "rules" that are true throughout our thinking and applied to almost all situations. They are the very basic assumptions we make about the world, others, and ourselves. They are so automatic that we often don't even stop to think about them. Core beliefs make up what we believe about reality and our self-identity—what we hold as important or meaningful, and what options or choices we see as available to us.

Core beliefs are the thoughts behind our thinking.

They are the thoughts that lead us from "That person makes me mad" to "He deserves to be hit," or from "I like the looks of that car" to "Therefore it's okay for me to steal it." Or they are the thoughts behind the thinking that takes us from "I should never have to feel bad" to "Therefore it's all right to use alcohol or drugs because I deserve to feel good." Your beliefs determine how you justify and explain your behavior. They are the story you tell yourself and others that makes it okay for you to rob, steal, assault, and use alcohol and drugs despite the consequences to yourself and your relationships.

Not all your core beliefs are distorted. Some of them help to protect you. They also help you to consider the needs and safety of others. Healthy core beliefs don't cause harm to others—they don't create victims.

EXERCISE 73 EXERCISE

Identifying Your Core Beliefs

➤ Write down the first thing that comes to your mind:

1. The world is _____

2. Other people are _____

3. Other people should try to _____

4. I try to be _____

5. The world would be better if _____

_____

6. The best way to get what you want is to _____

_____

7. I deserve _____

_____

8. If people try to stop me from getting what I want, then

_____

_____

"The Little Engine That Could"

Core beliefs are the thoughts behind your thinking. Remember the children's story called *The Little Engine That Could*? The story is about a small train engine that is asked to pull many freight cars filled with toys and candy across a mountain. The train's first engine had broken down and no other engines were willing to do the work. Though no one thought the little engine was powerful enough for the job, it volunteered to try. It started out by saying to itself, "I think I can. I think I can." It kept saying "I think I can" as it picked up speed and as it began the long, hard climb up the mountain. It continued to say it until it finally reached the top and could begin the easy trip down the other side.

What does this simple child's tale have to do with core beliefs? Let's work backward:

Question: What was the behavior?
Answer: Pulling the train over the mountain.

Question: What was the thought behind the behavior?
Answer: I think I can.

Question: What was the core belief behind the thought?
Answer: I believe that, with effort and determination, I can do more than others think I'm capable of doing.

Your core beliefs support your thinking, just like the rocks and earth underneath the ground support the world you live in. You don't see them, but they are there. You can also think of core beliefs as the framework of a big building—the girders and beams that make up the skeleton of the building—that you don't see but that keep the whole building from collapsing.

The same is true of your core beliefs. They are so automatic that we are often not even aware of their impact on our thinking and behavior. But by looking at your thinking distortions and criminal and addictive thinking, you can begin to identify which of your core beliefs cause harm to others—and to yourself.

Here are some examples of core beliefs.

View of the world:

- It's a dog-eat-dog world.

- Life is tough and then you die.

- The world should be just and fair.

- People get what they deserve out of life.

View of others:

- Everyone is out for themselves.

- Get them before they get you.

- Treat others as you'd want to be treated.

- Others are inferior to me.

- Others are here to meet my needs, or at least they should stay out of my way.

- If everyone else would get their act together, I would be fine.

- People are basically good.

View of self:

- I am above others and deserve respect at all times.

- Since I am special, I deserve special treatment.

- I can make a positive difference in people's lives.

- Rules aren't for me; I am entitled to break the rules.

- If people knew the real me, they would reject me.

- My feelings are always correct.

Based on your core beliefs, you develop certain strategies to make things go according to your thinking. But you—like most people—generally look at the world *through* your core beliefs. You seldom look *at* them. And you believe that everyone else in the world looks at things the way you do. For example, you probably think:

- Everybody in your situation would have done the things you did.

- Everybody uses because everybody in *your* world uses.

- If everybody had as hard a life as you, they'd commit crimes, too.

Sometimes things happen that go against what you believe are "just the way things are." When this is the case, you are much more likely to change or distort that information to fit what you already believe. Again, that's true for most people, not just criminals.

Criminals, however, have core beliefs that allow for and justify criminal behavior.

So when you believe it's a dog-eat-dog world and someone does something nice for you, you automatically think that person must be trying to con you. When people make you angry, you tell yourself you are justified in beating them up because "they asked for it" or "they should have known better" or "they simply got what they deserved."

A problem that many people, including criminals, have with their core beliefs is that they think everyone has the same core beliefs that they have. It's wrong to assume that our core beliefs are the same as everyone else's. Many of your life's conflicts happened because you tried to insist that everyone else shares your core beliefs. The world of your core beliefs is way too small. And that's one reason why your thought map has failed you: It doesn't tell you much about the larger world you live in. Your small, criminal core beliefs have kept you trapped in a small, criminal world.

One of the basic goals of treatment is to get you to look at, and question, some of your core beliefs. You need to look at the "rules" that you apply automatically across different situations. Doing so will cause you to react and behave in ways that create problems for yourself and others. As a result this examination is a very difficult thing to do.

How Core Beliefs Lead to
Thinking and Behavior

➤ Write your current offense below in the far right-hand column. Then review your answers to the questions in exercise 73. Use those answers as a guide to the core beliefs that seem to have a connection to your current offense. List them below in the far left-hand column.

In the middle column, write a thought that could come out of each of the core beliefs that would lead to committing your current offense.

Core beliefs   Specific thoughts

1. _____   _____

   _____   _____

2. _____   _____

                                    _____
   _____   _____   current offense
                                                          (behavior)

3. _____   _____

   _____   _____

The crime is the behavior. It resulted from specific thoughts like the ones you described above. The thoughts came out of your core beliefs about the world, others, and yourself.

Exercise 73 helped you start to become aware of your core beliefs. It will take you much more time and effort to identify your basic beliefs and to challenge them. Seeing what kinds of issues come up again and again in your Thinking Reports and what your thoughts are leading up to in those situations can help your thinking become more deliberate and less reactive.

If you have not already done so, you are now ready to start identifying the core beliefs (the thoughts behind your thoughts) that operate behind your criminal and addictive thinking patterns and to start adding core beliefs to your Thinking Reports. You are also ready to begin trying to think of replacement core beliefs—new beliefs—that might work better for you in recovery. Adding new beliefs may lead you to healthier, more rewarding thoughts and outcomes. Add this information to your Thinking Report on page 179.

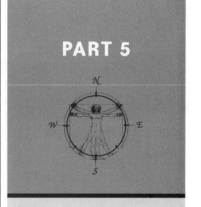

Criminality and Addiction on a Continuum

To review, there are four aspects of your criminal and addictive thinking. They are

1. thinking distortions
2. criminal thinking patterns
3. addictive thinking patterns
4. core beliefs

Now that you are beginning to understand your criminal and addictive thinking and how that thinking has gotten you into trouble, it's time to look at the big picture. Looking at the big picture will help you better see

1. where you are now

2. how you got here

3. where you're headed if you don't change your thinking

4. where you could go if you *do* change your thinking

The big picture is called the continuum of criminality and the continuum of addiction. As you learned earlier, a *continuum* is a line that represents movement from one place to another (and sometimes back again).

As both a criminal and an addict, you are living your life on both the continuum of criminality *and* the continuum of addiction. While you may move back and forth a little bit, for the most part you have been moving in just one direction—getting worse.

The Continuum of Criminality

The four "stops" or stages on the continuum of criminality are the following:

- being responsible

- being irresponsible (noncriminal)

- being irresponsible (criminal)

- being an extreme criminal

Figure 17

THE CONTINUUM OF CRIMINALITY

Responsible	Irresponsible (noncriminal)	Irresponsible (criminal)	Extreme Criminal

Each of these stages is identified by certain behavior and thinking tendencies. Here are the tendencies:

Responsible

____ Has a pattern of accepting responsibility at home, at work, and in society

____ Has a lifestyle based on hard work and fulfilling obligations

____ Has consideration of others

____ Gets self-respect and the respect of others through achievement

____ Desires to violate may happen, but they disappear without having to make a conscious choice

____ Does not violate the rights or property of others

____ Makes choices that are in the best interests of both self and others

____ Trusts the judgment of others

Irresponsible (noncriminal)

____ Accepts only a small amount of responsibility and makes excuses

____ Willing to lie, manipulate, and intimidate to get his way

____ Generally unreliable and chronically late—may perform poorly at work

____ Often fails to carry out promises and obligations at home

____ Expects to fail and makes only halfhearted attempts

____ Lacks goal-oriented direction

Irresponsible (criminal)

____ Accepts responsibility only when backed into a corner but then fights it all the way

____ Has the thinking patterns of the extreme criminal but with less extensive crime patterns

____ Is a minor violator who rarely gets caught

____ Is very secretive and isolated from others

____ Feels successful because he hasn't been caught for much of his criminal activity

____ Has desires to violate but doesn't most of the time

____ Without restraints, will commit violations previously only thought about

____ Moves away from family or to different city or area to decrease restraints (be more free to offend) and to be more unknown (incognito)

Extreme Criminal

____ Accepts little or no responsibility

____ Has a continuous flow of criminal thoughts

____ Has concern only for self—defends self at all costs

____ Sees self as a good person, not a criminal

____ Seeks to promote self at the expense of others

____ Exploits relationships for self-profit

____ Criticizes others, blames others, and claims injustice when things don't go his way

____ Sees being nice as a weakness

____ Is overconfident and grandiose—won't stop trying to beat the system

Where Are You on the
Continuum of Criminality?

➤ Review the four "stops" on the continuum of criminality. Place an X beside the items that apply to you. Think about what led up to the offense that brought you behind bars the last time. *Be honest with yourself.* Learning to tell yourself the truth about yourself is the first step in your recovery from both addiction and criminality.

➤ Looking back, where do you think you were on the continuum of criminality when you were incarcerated this last time?

_____

➤ Why do you think that? Which characteristics of that "stop" on the continuum describe you especially well?

_____

_____

_____

➤ Do you think you are still in the same "stop" on the continuum of criminality as you were when you were locked up this most recent time? Why or why not?

_____

_____

_____

The Life Course of the Criminal-Addict and the Noncriminal-Nonaddict

How did you happen to become a criminal-addict? Figure 18a shows the life course of the noncriminal-nonaddict and Figure 18b shows the life course of the criminal-addict.

Figure 18a

THE NONCRIMINAL-NONADDICT LIFE COURSE

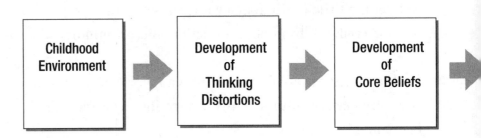

Figure 18b

THE CRIMINAL-ADDICT LIFE COURSE

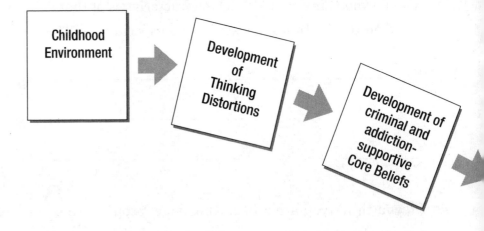

As you can see, everyone comes from a childhood environment that includes family, community, and physical and material conditions. For some people, those conditions are nurturing, safe, and bountiful. For others they are cruel, dangerous, and deprived. Most people's childhood environments fall somewhere in between those two extremes.

You may think that you're a criminal and addict because your childhood was particularly hard. Growing up in a cruel, dangerous, or deprived environment may

Development of noncriminal and nonaddict thinking patterns → *The noncriminal/nonaddict life course*

contribute toward the decision to take a criminal life path or turn to chemicals. Resentments, anger at the unfairness of life, and fear for survival poison the mind and can direct a person toward disconnecting from society. But that disconnection is also a *choice. And it is a choice you made.*

Not everybody made that choice. As you learned in exercise 22 on page 95, not everyone who grew up where you did and experienced what you did became a criminal or an addict. Most, in fact, did not—because they *chose* not to.

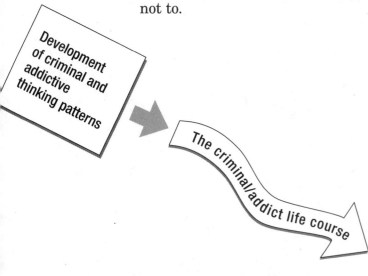

Development of criminal and addictive thinking patterns → *The criminal/addict life course*

Why did you choose crime and drugs? Because you developed core beliefs that supported criminal and addictive thinking patterns. It is your criminal and addictive thinking patterns that sent you on the downward slide into criminality and addiction.

After all, there are problems, and there is how you *handle* problems. The choices you make about how to handle your problems can be either criminal or noncriminal; courageous and straightforward or an escape into drugs or alcohol.

Understanding what happened when you left the non-criminal-nonaddict life will help you better understand how to stop the downward slide and begin to move back up into recovery and responsible living.

The Progression of Criminal Development

The continuum of criminality helps show you where you are in your criminal life. It helps describe you as you are. It does not show you how you got there or where you're headed. The steps you took into a criminal life can also be seen in stages. Your movement into the criminal life is a downward slide or progression. Again, there are four stages of this progression. Each has identifying characteristics, behaviors, and ways of thinking.

The progression of criminal development is shown on the next page. You can see that the five stages of criminal development are

1. pre-criminal stage

2. early criminal stage

3. middle criminal stage

4. late criminal stage

5. denial stage

Figure 19

THE PROGRESSION OF CRIMINAL DEVELOPMENT

Pre-Criminal Stage

__ Arrests for nuisance and status-type offenses (show-off, to get a "rep")

__ Vandalism, larceny, burglary, and auto theft are popular crimes

__ Crimes are committed in the company of groups or gangs

__ Peer pressure is an important influence in the decision to offend

__ Crimes are committed for excitement (though less severe crimes than in later stages)

__ The best chance to change happens here (about half in this stage drop out of the criminal life)

Early Criminal Stage

__ Greater investment of time, energy, and interest in crime

__ Thrills, status, and peer acceptance are no longer important reasons for committing crimes

__ Contemplate crime as a career or lifestyle

__ Frequency of crime drops, but the severity increases; the desire for power and control over others, greed, and an "I don't care" attitude increase

__ Desire for money to get drugs and nonessential material things increases

Middle Criminal Stage

__ Committed to a criminal way of life

__ Anger and resentment become primary motivations for crime

__ Increasing concern with power and control over others

__ Lowest frequency and highest severity of crime

__ Count on the "Big Score" to make everything all right

__ Criminal lifestyle frenzy is very dangerous to self and others— greater and more risks are taken

Late Criminal Stage

__ Decreased physical strength, stamina, and activity

__ Less concern with material things and awareness of crime as a "no-win" way of life

__ Fear of growing old and dying behind bars

__ Burnout: wearing down due to age and the accumulation of negative consequences

__ Maturity: re-evaluation of life goals and priorities (while burnout is expected, maturity may or may not happen)

Denial Stage

This is a "bottoming out" or pre-recovery stage. Denial is part of every stage in the entire downward progression of criminality and addiction, but it is also the state in which recovery must begin.

__ Still doesn't recognize a problem and is resistant to change—is in full denial

__ Continues to minimize behavior by comparing self to others who are worse or behaviors that are worse

__ Still rationalizes behavior by putting a positive spin on it, dismissing it as history, or portraying self as the victim

> It's a steep slope from the pre-criminal stage to the late criminal stage. You start at the top and it carries you swiftly to the bottom. Recovery can begin at any stage in the process. You don't have to hit rock-bottom first. Breaking through the denial prevents you from reaching or staying at the bottom.

Here are the characteristics that define each stage:

Pre-Criminal Stage

____ Arrests for nuisance and status-type offenses (show-off, to get a "rep")

____ Vandalism, larceny, burglary, and auto theft are popular crimes

____ Crimes are committed in the company of groups or gangs

____ Peer pressure is an important influence in the decision to offend

____ Crimes are committed for excitement (though less severe crimes than in later stages)

____ The best chance to change happens here (about half in this stage drop out of the criminal life)

Early Criminal Stage

____ Greater investment of time, energy, and interest in crime

____ Thrills, status, and peer acceptance are no longer important reasons for committing crimes

____ Contemplate crime as a career or lifestyle

____ Frequency of crimes drop, but the severity increases; the desire for power and control over others, greed, and "I don't care" attitude increase

____ Desire for money to get drugs and nonessential material things increases

Middle Criminal Stage

____ Committed to a criminal way of life

____ Anger and resentment become primary motivations for crime

____ Increasing concern with power and control over others

____ Lowest frequency and highest severity of crime

____ Count on the "Big Score" to make everything all right

____ Criminal lifestyle frenzy is very dangerous to self and others—greater and more risks are taken

Late Criminal Stage

____ Decreased physical strength, stamina, and activity

____ Less concern with material things and awareness of crime as a "no-win" way of life

____ Fear of growing old and dying behind bars.

____ Burnout: wearing down due to age and the accumulation of negative consequences

____ Maturity: re-evaluation of life goals and priorities (While burnout is expected, maturity may or may not happen.)

Denial Stage

This is a "bottoming out" or prerecovery stage. Denial is part of every stage in the entire downward progression of criminality and addiction, but it is also the state in which recovery must begin.

____ Still doesn't recognize a problem and is resistant to change—is in full denial

____ Continues to minimize behavior by comparing self to others who are worse or behaviors that are worse

____ Still rationalizes behavior by putting a positive spin on it, dismissing it as history, or portraying self as the victim

What Stage of Your
Criminal Development Are You In?

➤ You've already identified where you think you are on the criminal continuum. The progression of criminal development tells you a little bit more about how you moved into your criminal career. Reread the characteristics of the five stages on pages 238–239 and put an **X** by the ones that apply to you.

➤ Judging from the characteristics that you checked, what stage in the development of your criminal career were you in when you were locked up this last time?

_____

_____

➤ Why do you think that? Which characteristics in that stage most describe your criminal life?

_____

_____

_____

_____

_____

_____

Look again at figure 19. Notice the circle at the bottom of the line that is moving downward into criminality from left to right.

That circle represents the opportunity for change.

It's the chance you have right now to turn your life around and start back up again. No matter what stage you are at in the progression of your criminal development, you can place that circle right where you are now and begin the climb toward responsible living.

The Progression of Criminal Recovery

Just as there are stages in the progression of criminal development, there are also stages in criminal recovery. You can see by looking at figure 20 (on the next page) that it doesn't happen overnight. It will take time and effort to move through the stages toward building a life that won't bring you back to where you are right now. But it can be done. The stages of criminal recovery show you the path.

Figure 20 shows the five stages in the progression of criminal recovery. They are

1. bargaining stage

2. early recovery stage

3. middle recovery stage

4. late recovery stage

5. maintenance stage

You can begin the climb toward responsible living.

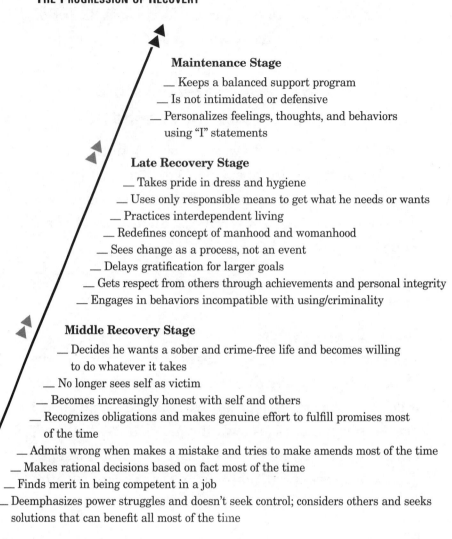

Figure 20

THE PROGRESSION OF RECOVERY

Maintenance Stage

__ Keeps a balanced support program

__ Is not intimidated or defensive

__ Personalizes feelings, thoughts, and behaviors using "I" statements

Late Recovery Stage

__ Takes pride in dress and hygiene

__ Uses only responsible means to get what he needs or wants

__ Practices interdependent living

__ Redefines concept of manhood and womanhood

__ Sees change as a process, not an event

__ Delays gratification for larger goals

__ Gets respect from others through achievements and personal integrity

__ Engages in behaviors incompatible with using/criminality

Middle Recovery Stage

__ Decides he wants a sober and crime-free life and becomes willing to do whatever it takes

__ No longer sees self as victim

__ Becomes increasingly honest with self and others

__ Recognizes obligations and makes genuine effort to fulfill promises most of the time

__ Admits wrong when makes a mistake and tries to make amends most of the time

__ Makes rational decisions based on fact most of the time

__ Finds merit in being competent in a job

__ Deemphasizes power struggles and doesn't seek control; considers others and seeks solutions that can benefit all most of the time

Early Recovery Stage

__ Intention to change plus *some* effort to do so

__ Asks questions, though usually the wrong questions, such as, "Why is the world out to get me?"

__ Seeks to control anger, criminal impulse, and impulse to use alcohol or drugs by force of will

__ Does the minimum to get by (false compliance) rather than fully committing to a sober, crime-free lifestyle

__ May not see need for more effective action and get stuck at this stage

__ May begin to understand that recovery involves daily choices that support not using and not committing crimes

The goal of the progression of recovery is to move on up the slope. You begin at the bottom—the bargaining stage. Here, the decision to change is made.

Bargaining Stage

This is a pre-recovery stage. Bargaining may be part of the downward progression of criminality and addiction, but it is also the beginning of an awareness that change is needed.

__ General awareness of a problem but not sure what it is

__ Still tends to project the problem onto other people or external circumstances

__ Thinks about need for change, but only "sometime in the future"

__ Has a magical or wishful view of change—that it will just happen without personal effort

__ Thinks more about what is comfortable than what needs to be done

__ Makes external changes such as the "geographical cure" (moving to a new place to escape past behaviors) in mistaken belief it will fix everything

__ Makes deals, such as only weekend use or only property crime or will sell but not use

Here are the characteristics that define these stages:

Bargaining Stage

This is a pre-recovery stage. Bargaining may be part of the downward progression of criminality and addiction, but it is also the beginning of an awareness that change is needed.

____ General awareness of a problem but not sure what it is

____ Still tends to project the problem onto other people or external circumstances

____ Thinks about need for change, but only "sometime in the future"

____ Has a magical or wishful view of change—that it will just happen without personal effort

____ Thinks more about what is comfortable than what needs to be done

____ Makes external changes such as the "geographical cure" (moving to a new place to escape past behaviors) in mistaken belief it will fix everything

____ Makes deals, such as only weekend use or only property crime or will sell but not use

Early Recovery Stage

____ Intention to change plus *some* effort to do so

____ Asks questions, though usually the wrong questions, such as, "Why is the world out to get me?"

____ Seeks to control anger, criminal impulse, and the impulse to use alcohol or drugs by force of will

____ Does the minimum to get by (false compliance) rather than fully committing to a sober, crime-free lifestyle

____ May not see need for more effective action and get stuck at this stage

____ May begin to understand that recovery involves daily choices that support not using and not committing crimes

Middle Recovery Stage

____ Decides he wants a sober and crime-free life and becomes willing to do whatever it takes

____ No longer sees self as victim

____ Becomes increasingly honest with self and others.

____ Recognizes obligations and makes genuine effort to fulfill promises most of the time

____ Admits wrong when makes a mistake and tries to make amends most of the time

____ Makes rational decisions based on fact most of the time

____ Finds merit in being competent in a job

____ Deemphasizes power struggles and doesn't seek control; considers others and seeks solutions that can benefit all most of the time

Late Recovery Stage

____ Takes pride in dress and hygiene

____ Uses only responsible means to get what he needs or wants

____ Practices interdependent living

____ Redefines concept of manhood and womanhood

____ Sees change as a process, not an event

____ Delays gratification for larger goals

____ Gets respect from others through achievements and personal integrity

____ Engages in behaviors incompatible with using or criminality

Maintenance Stage

____ Keeps a balanced support program

____ Is not intimidated or defensive

____ Personalizes feelings, thoughts, and behaviors using "I" statements

The time and effort your recovery from criminality takes depends on the following:

1. where you are in your progression of criminal development (the downward slide)

2. how committed you are to turning the course of your life around

3. other factors

There will be setbacks; there will be frustrations. How difficult your recovery will be also depends on how well you deal with these setbacks and frustrations.

Figure 21
THE PROGRESSION OF CRIMINAL DEVELOPMENT AND RECOVERY

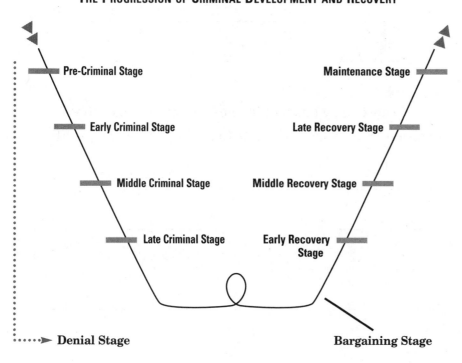

Pre-Criminal Stage

Early Criminal Stage

Middle Criminal Stage

Late Criminal Stage

Denial Stage

Maintenance Stage

Late Recovery Stage

Middle Recovery Stage

Early Recovery Stage

Bargaining Stage

Have You Made the Decision to Recover from Criminality?

Remember, the circle at the bottom of figure 21 represents the decision to turn your life around, to seek recovery. Think about whether you have really made that decision.

➤ Place an **X** next to the statement that is most true for you.

____ **Yes,** I have made the decision to turn my life around.

____ **No,** I have not yet committed to leaving the criminal life.

➤ If you chose yes, what choices will you make to turn your life around?

_____

_____

_____

➤ If you chose no, what will it take for you to make that decision? Why don't you want to give up the criminal life?

_____

_____

_____

_____

What Stage of Your
Criminal Recovery Are You In?

➤ What stage of your recovery from criminality are you in?

_____

_____

_____

➤ Why do you think you are in that stage?

_____

_____

_____

➤ How does your thinking and behavior reflect this?

_____

_____

_____

The Continuum of Addiction

Just as there is a continuum of criminality, there is also a continuum of addiction. It also has four "stops" or stages. They are

- responsible use
- irresponsible use
- abuse/early addiction
- advanced addiction

Figure 22
THE CONTINUUM OF ADDICTION

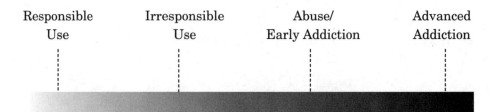

| Responsible Use | Irresponsible Use | Abuse/ Early Addiction | Advanced Addiction |

Each of these "stops" on the continuum has certain features:

Responsible Use

____ Occasional alcohol use in social settings

____ Does not drink to get drunk

____ Does not violate the law to use (does not use illegal substances)

____ Does not drive after drinking

____ Does not go out of way to get a drink

____ Does not lie and is not secretive about drinking

Irresponsible Use

____ Occasionally drinks to excess

____ Uses illegal substances to get high once in a while

____ Sometimes drives after using

____ Sometimes uses to feel better, to relieve stress, or to alter unhappy or sad feelings

____ Provides illegal substances to others or alcohol to minors to have company in using

____ Underage drinking

Abuse/Early Addiction

____ Regularly uses to get drunk or high, even before work or family events

____ Uses almost every time when feels bad

____ Sometimes violates own morals and values in order to use or when using

____ Associates almost entirely with irresponsible users, abusers, and addicts

____ Makes excuses and lies about using

____ Has frequent problems with family and work because of using

____ Creates rituals around using and buys many products associated with using

____ Neglects healthy diet and develops irregular sleep patterns

____ Tries the "geographical cure," moves away in attempt to start over

Advanced Addiction

____ Has powerful cravings for drugs or alcohol and a need to relieve them

____ Has unpleasant withdrawal symptoms (with alcohol and most—but not all—other drugs) if can't get supply or tries to stop

____ Life revolves entirely around using (loss of other interests)

____ Isolates self from most or all friends and family members

____ Violates own morals and values regularly in order to use

____ Is full of undefined fears; has irrational suspicions of others

EXERCISE **79** EXERCISE

Where Are You on the Continuum of Addiction?

Review the four "stops" on the continuum of addiction on pages 248–250. Place a mark beside the ones that apply to you, especially to your life before you were incarcerated this last time.

➤ Where do you think you were on the continuum of addiction when you were incarcerated this last time?

_____

_____

_____

➤ Why do you think that? Which characteristics of that "stop" on the continuum describe you especially well?

_____

_____

_____

The Progression of Addiction

The continuum of addiction helps you see where you are in your addiction, but it doesn't show how you got there. Just as there was a progression of stages that you followed into criminality, there is also a progression of stages into addiction. These stages are:

1. use

2. early stage

3. middle stage (crucial phase)

4. late stage (chronic phase)

5. denial stage

These stages also come with identifying characteristics, behaviors, and ways of thinking. The progression of addiction development is shown on the next page.

As figure 23 on page 252 shows, here are the characteristics that define each stage:

Use

____ Experimentation

____ Uses in the company of peers

____ Moderate or occasional use

____ Social or recreational use

____ Moderate and frequent use

____ Moderate but habitual use

____ Occasional use for "kicks" or "thrills"

Early Stage

____ Pattern of amount and frequency of use which, if continued, has high potential of leading to abuse and addiction

____ Uses to relieve stress, to make self feel better

Figure 23
THE PROGRESSION OF ADDICTION DEVELOPMENT

Use
__ Experimentation
__ Uses in the company of peers
__ Moderate or occasional use
__ Social or recreational use
__ Moderate and frequent use
__ Moderate but habitual use
__ Occasional use for "kicks" or "thrills"

Early Stage
__ Pattern of amount and frequency of use which, if continued, has high potential of leading to abuse and addiction
__ Uses to relieve stress, to make self feel better
__ Frequent use for "kicks" or "thrills"
__ Uses with intent to get high or drunk
__ Spree use (heavy use over more than one day)
__ Occasional use of excessive amounts to extreme intoxication

Middle Stage (Crucial Phase)
__ Amount and frequency of use interferes with "normal" functioning in society
__ Regular spree use, use for "thrills," and intent to get high or drunk
__ Increasing use of excessive amounts to extreme intoxication
__ Habitual use of excessive amounts to extreme intoxication
__ Continued use despite experiencing negative reactions and consequences
__ Lack of awareness of the degree of impairment while under the influence
__ Plans to change use patterns but is easily drawn into old patterns
__ Increase in tolerance—takes greater amount of the drug to achieve the high

Late Stage (Chronic Phase)
__ Tries to stop using but can't
__ Uses alone and hides use
__ Continues to use despite harmful consequences
__ Preoccupation, or obsession, with the drug
__ Serious deterioration of physical and mental health
__ Decrease in tolerance—lesser amount of the drug causes greater loss of control (with alcohol and some other drugs)
__ Loses control of most aspects of life
__ Bottoms out with loss of ability to function in the world

Denial Stage

This is a "bottoming out" or pre-recovery stage. Denial is part of every stage in the entire downward progression of criminality and addiction, but it is also the state in which recovery must begin.

__ Still doesn't recognize a problem and is resistant to change—is in full denial

__ Continues to minimize behavior by comparing self to others who are worse or behaviors that are worse

__ Still rationalizes behavior by putting a positive spin on it, dismissing it as history, or portraying self as the victim

It's a steep slope from the beginning stage of addiction to the late stage. You start at the top and it carries you swiftly to the bottom. Recovery can begin at any stage in the process. You don't have to hit rock-bottom first. Breaking through the denial prevents you from reaching or staying at the bottom.

____ Frequent use for "kicks" or "thrills"

____ Uses with intent to get high or drunk

____ Spree use (heavy use over more than one day)

____ Occasional use of excessive amounts to extreme intoxication

Middle Stage (Crucial Phase)

____ Amount and frequency of use interferes with "normal" functioning in society

____ Regular spree use, use for "thrills," and intent to get high or drunk

____ Increasing use of excessive amounts to extreme intoxication

____ Habitual use of excessive amounts to extreme intoxication

____ Continued use despite experiencing negative reactions and consequences

____ Lack of awareness of the degree of impairment while under the influence

____ Plans to change use patterns but is easily drawn into old patterns

____ Increase in tolerance—takes greater amount of the drug to achieve the high

Late Stage (Chronic Phase)

____ Tries to stop using but can't

____ Uses alone and hides use

____ Continues to use despite harmful consequences

____ Preoccupation, or obsession, with the drug

____ Serious deterioration of physical and mental health

____ Decrease in tolerance—lesser amount of the drug causes greater loss of control (with alcohol and some other drugs)

____ Loses control of most aspects of life

____ Bottoms out with loss of ability to function in the world

Denial Stage

This is a "bottoming out" or pre-recovery stage. Denial is part of every stage in the entire downward progression of criminality and addiction, but it is also the state in which recovery must begin.

____ Still doesn't recognize a problem and is resistant to change—is in full denial

____ Continues to minimize behavior by comparing self to others who are worse or behaviors that are worse

____ Still rationalizes behavior by putting a positive spin on it, dismissing it as history, or portraying self as the victim

What Stage of Your Addiction Development Are You In?

➤ You've already identified where you think you are on the addiction continuum. The progression of addiction development tells you a little bit more about *how* you moved into your habitual chemical use. Review the characteristics of the five stages on pages 251 and 253–254 and put an **X** by the ones that apply to you.

➤ Judging from the characteristics that you marked, what stage in the development of your addiction were you in when you were locked up this last time?

_____

➤ Why do you think that? Which characteristics in that stage most describe how you used chemicals before you were locked up this most recent time?

_____

_____

_____

_____

_____

The Progression of Addiction Recovery

If you look again at figure 23, the progression of addiction development, you see that it also has a circle. As with the progression of criminal development, the circle represents the possibility—and opportunity—of changing the downward direction of your progression into addiction and moving back upward into recovery. And again, no matter where you are on the progression of addiction, your decision to seek recovery creates the circle and changes your direction.

Figure 24 on the following page shows the five stages in the progression of addiction recovery. They are

1. bargaining stage

2. early recovery stage

3. middle recovery stage

4. late recovery stage

5. maintenance stage

Here are the characteristics that define these stages:

Bargaining Stage

This is a pre-recovery stage. Bargaining may be part of the downward progression of criminality and addiction, but it is also the beginning of an awareness that change is needed.

_____ General awareness of a problem but not sure what it is

_____ Still tends to project the problem onto other people or external circumstances

_____ Thinks about need for change, but only "sometime in the future"

_____ Has a magical or wishful view of change—that it will just happen without personal effort

Figure 24
THE PROGRESSION OF RECOVERY

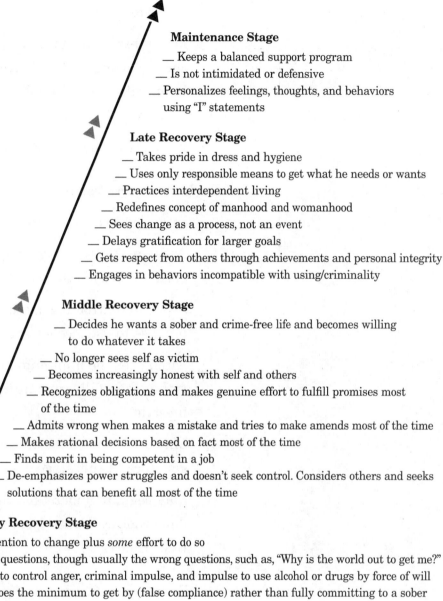

The goal of the progression of recovery is to move on up the slope. You begin at the bottom—the bargaining stage. Here, the decision to change is made.

Maintenance Stage
— Keeps a balanced support program
— Is not intimidated or defensive
— Personalizes feelings, thoughts, and behaviors using "I" statements

Late Recovery Stage
— Takes pride in dress and hygiene
— Uses only responsible means to get what he needs or wants
— Practices interdependent living
— Redefines concept of manhood and womanhood
— Sees change as a process, not an event
— Delays gratification for larger goals
— Gets respect from others through achievements and personal integrity
— Engages in behaviors incompatible with using/criminality

Middle Recovery Stage
— Decides he wants a sober and crime-free life and becomes willing to do whatever it takes
— No longer sees self as victim
— Becomes increasingly honest with self and others
— Recognizes obligations and makes genuine effort to fulfill promises most of the time
— Admits wrong when makes a mistake and tries to make amends most of the time
— Makes rational decisions based on fact most of the time
— Finds merit in being competent in a job
— De-emphasizes power struggles and doesn't seek control. Considers others and seeks solutions that can benefit all most of the time

Early Recovery Stage
— Intention to change plus *some* effort to do so
— Asks questions, though usually the wrong questions, such as, "Why is the world out to get me?"
— Seeks to control anger, criminal impulse, and impulse to use alcohol or drugs by force of will
— Often does the minimum to get by (false compliance) rather than fully committing to a sober and crime-free lifestyle
— May not see need for more effective action and may get stuck at this stage
— May begin to understand that recovery involves daily choices that support not using and not committing crimes

Bargaining Stage
This is a pre-recovery stage. Bargaining may be part of the downward progression of criminality and addiction, but it is also the beginning of an awareness that change is needed.
— General awareness of a problem but not sure what it is
— Still tends to project the problem onto other people or external circumstances
— Thinks about need for change, but only "sometime in the future"
— Has a magical or wishful view of change—that it will just happen without personal effort
— Thinks more about what is comfortable than what needs to be done
— Makes external changes such as the "geographical cure" (moving to a new place to escape past behaviors) in mistaken belief it will fix everything
— Makes deals, such as only weekend use or only property crime or will sell but not use

____ Thinks more about what is comfortable than what needs to be done

____ Makes external changes such as the "geographical cure" (moving to a new place to escape past behaviors) in mistaken belief it will fix everything

____ Makes deals, such as only weekend use or only property crime or will sell but not use

Early Recovery Stage

____ Intention to change plus *some* effort to do so

____ Asks questions, though usually the wrong questions, such as, "Why is the world out to get me?"

____ Seeks to control anger, criminal impulse, and the impulse to use alcohol or drugs by force of will

____ Often does the minimum to get by (false compliance) rather than fully committing to a sober and crime-free lifestyle

____ May not see need for more effective action and may get stuck at this stage

____ May begin to understand that recovery involves daily choices that support not using and not committing crimes

Middle Recovery Stage

____ Decides he wants a sober and crime-free life and becomes willing to do whatever it takes

____ No longer sees self as victim

____ Becomes increasingly honest with self and others

____ Recognizes obligations and makes genuine effort to fulfill promises most of the time

____ Admits wrong when makes a mistake and tries to make amends most of the time

___ Makes rational decisions based on fact most of the time

___ Finds merit in being competent in a job

___ De-emphasizes power struggles and doesn't seek control. Considers others and seeks solutions that can benefit all most of the time

Late Recovery Stage

___ Takes pride in dress and hygiene

___ Uses only responsible means to get what he needs or wants

___ Practices interdependent living

___ Redefines concept of manhood and womanhood

___ Sees change as a process, not an event

___ Delays gratification for larger goals

___ Gets respect from others through achievements and personal integrity

___ Engages in behaviors incompatible with using or criminality

Maintenance Stage

___ Keeps a balanced support program

___ Is not intimidated or defensive

___ Personalizes feelings, thoughts, and behaviors using "I" statements

As figure 24 on page 257 shows, recovery from addiction, like recovery from criminality, is also a progression. Over time, you will build a path to sobriety brick by brick, moving through the various stages toward reaching your life potential.

And again, the progression of recovery from addiction begins with the circle at the bottom, the decision to turn your life around and try something new: recovery.

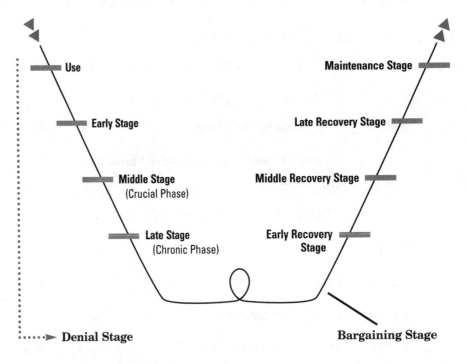

Figure 25
THE PROGRESSION OF ADDICTION DEVELOPMENT AND RECOVERY

Use

Early Stage

Middle Stage
(Crucial Phase)

Late Stage
(Chronic Phase)

Denial Stage

Maintenance Stage

Late Recovery Stage

Middle Recovery Stage

Early Recovery
Stage

Bargaining Stage

No matter where you are on the progression of addiction, your decision to seek recovery creates the circle and changes your direction.

Have You Made the Decision
to Recover from Addiction?

Remember, the circle at the bottom of figure 25 represents the decision to turn your life around, to seek recovery. Think about whether you have really made that decision.

➤ Place an **X** next to the statement that is most true for you.

____ **Yes,** I have made the decision to turn my life around.

____ **No,** I have not yet committed to leaving the using life.

➤ If you chose yes, what choices will you make to turn your life around?

_____

_____

_____

➤ If you chose no, what will it take for you to make that decision? Why don't you want to give up the using life?

_____

_____

_____

What Stage of Your
Addiction Recovery Are You In?

➤ What stage of your recovery from addiction are you in? (If you don't think you've started yet, write "Haven't started.")

_____

_____

_____

➤ Why do you think you are in that stage?

_____

_____

_____

➤ How has your thinking and behavior shown this?

_____

_____

_____

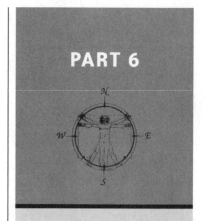

Learning to Think about Your Behavior

We've discussed thinking distortions, criminal and addictive thinking patterns, and core beliefs, and we've shown how all these can lead to irresponsible behavior. Remember, your *behavior* is the result of your *thinking*. Earlier in this workbook, you explored your habits of thinking. Now you'll look at some of your habits of behavior that resulted from that thinking.

Behavior can be responsible, irresponsible (legal, but potentially damaging to you or others), or criminal (violating others in ways society prohibits by law). As we've seen with the continuum of criminality, a lot of irresponsible thinking and behavior and criminal thinking and behavior sit right next to each other—they're only slightly different. But since you are reading this in a treatment program behind bars, your thinking and behavior probably fits into either the "irresponsible and criminal" or "extreme criminal" stop on the continuum of criminality.

You have seriously broken the law at least once and perhaps many, many more times.

In fact, the odds are that you have done so much irresponsible behavior, both criminal and noncriminal, that you have developed patterns of behavior. These behavior strategies have worked well for you in manipulating, intimidating, controlling, and violating others. You have used these behaviors so often and so consistently that they have become habits for you. These habits of criminal and addictive behavior are called *tactics.* Because they are habits, you use these criminal and addictive tactics in almost everything you do. You are probably using them in this treatment program.

The use of criminal and addictive tactics is a habit of behavior you will have to change in order to recover from both your criminality and your alcohol and drug use. To change these habits and recover, you will need to understand the thinking behind the tactics—why you do what you do.

Tactics

Tactics are planned behavior strategies and approaches intended to achieve a goal.

Criminal and Addictive Tactics

You use criminal and addictive tactics as a survival mechanism. You use them to avoid restrictions. You use them to get what you think you want. You use them to get people off your case or to avoid being held accountable for your behavior. And you also use them to avoid feeling put down or disrespected by others.

Who Uses Tactics?

Who uses tactics? Pretty much everybody. Generals, salespeople, parents, athletes, teachers, business managers, therapists, and others use tactics. Tactics are simply behaviors that are meant to get things done.

When responsible people use responsible tactics, they are intending to accomplish something helpful and worthwhile for themselves, their families, or their communities. The key is that they are not willing to use tactics in a way that violates the rights of others.

When irresponsible people use irresponsible tactics, they are trying to get something for themselves without earning it. They hide their true motives to take advantage of others and avoid responsibility.

When criminals use criminal tactics, they are trying to avoid being held accountable. They want to promote their criminal and addictive life—to get what you think they are entitled to or to avoid the feelings of zero state.

Avoiding and Escaping the Zero State

Remember the discussion of the criminal's and addict's zero state on pages 195–196? The biggest fear of all is falling into the zero state. You don't want to appear weak or indecisive or not in control. The zero state can result when others see your irresponsible thinking and behavior. It makes you feel worthless, empty, nothing—like you barely even exist.

You desperately try to avoid the zero state because you can't stand being in it. Criminal and addictive tactics help you avoid it. Once in the zero state, you desperately try to get out by using criminal and addictive tactics.

Fulfilling Your Sense of Entitlement

It is very important to remember that criminal and addictive tactics are not used just to escape or avoid the zero state. They are also used as the result of a powerful sense of entitlement—"I deserve to have whatever I want" or "I deserve to always feel good." Either way, tactics are a way to get what you want when you want it and to keep others from getting in your way.

How You Use Tactics

Criminal and addictive tactics are divided into these three types of strategies:

1. avoidance
2. diversion
3. aggression

You use *avoidance strategies* to escape responsibility, to keep a low profile so you won't have to put out effort or be exposed, and to manipulate others to get what you want.

You use *diversion strategies* to confuse others, to direct attention away from yourself or from the important issues, and to avoid exposure by keeping those around you distracted and focused on other things.

You use *aggression strategies* to attack, intimidate, and undermine the efforts of others. You actively try to create chaos by stirring up conflict, resentment, and other hard feelings.

You use avoidance strategies to escape responsibility.

The use of all three types of criminal and addictive tactics is the source of your feelings of criminal excitement and power. These strategies fuel your anger, resentment, and sense of entitlement. They help you deny the need for change by helping you deny your criminal and addictive thinking patterns, thinking distortions, and faulty core beliefs. They prevent you from setting goals for change.

Most criminals and addicts use all the tactics but in different orders. For example, you may prefer avoidance strategies, but if you run through all the avoidance tactics in a situation and they aren't working, you may flip over to diversion strategies. If those don't work, you'll try aggression strategies, and so on. Each person has his favorite tactics that he uses most often, but every criminal and addict is ready and willing to use any tactic that works in a situation.

For all these reasons, it is important that you understand one thing about your habits of behavior: *As a criminal and addictive thinker, you cannot make progress in treatment until you give up the excitement and power of using these criminal and addictive tactics and committing crimes or getting high.* And that has to start right now, in treatment. The first step in dealing with your use of criminal tactics is to name the tactics you use and learn to see them in your behavior. Then you can begin adding your tactics to your Thinking Reports.

Why is this just the first step? Because although understanding is crucial to change, it is not change. As your understanding of your use of tactics grows, you will begin the real work of recovery: letting go of old, irresponsible habits of living and substituting new, responsible ones *(new behaviors)* that will help you get along better in the world.

Avoidance Strategies

Here are the seven basic criminal and addictive tactics you use to get away with irresponsible thinking and behavior by avoidance:

1. lying by omission or commission (passive and active lying)

2. being deliberately vague

3. staying silent to avoid notice

4. false compliance

    a. compliance without commitment

    b. passive resistance compliance

5. playing dumb

6. selective memory and attention

7. minimizing (trivializing)

TACTIC 1:

Lying by Omission or Commission

Lying by omission or commission means misleading others by hiding the truth or telling half-truths (lying by omission, or passive lying) or misleading them by telling them things that are not true (lying by commission, or active lying). One is not better or worse than the other: A lie is a lie. You use lies to avoid getting caught, to hold power over others (withholding information can be powerful), to avoid accountability, and to continue your lifestyle.

You are lying by *omission* when you

- believe only you know what is important to disclose and what isn't

- disclose only the information that benefits you while withholding other important information, often by leaving out important details

- say "I don't know" or "I don't remember" when pressured for details; you do this as a way of avoiding accountability or an uncomfortable situation when in fact you *do* know

- use lead-in phrases like "to tell the truth" or "to be perfectly honest," usually a sure tip-off that you're withholding something

- twist facts and distort situations by shifting the emphasis onto minor facts while omitting crucial parts of the story

You are lying by *commission* when you

- make up stories to cover yourself and put others off the track

- deny to yourself or others what you know to be true

- believe that the truth works against your best interests and act accordingly

- distort, invent, turn upside down, or deny facts

TACTIC 2:

Being Deliberately Vague

Being deliberately vague means distorting the truth by fudging details, being intentionally uncertain of times and places, and trying to answer questions with wishy-washy generalities. Frequently claiming "I don't know" or "I can't remember" is one way of being deliberately vague. You use this tactic so you don't get pinned down. It's another way you avoid accountability and refuse to make a commitment to recovery. You think that vague statements will be enough to get people off your back without your having to confront your thinking and behavior and make changes. And you think that if others don't call you on it, then that's their problem. At least you didn't have to lie to them, and you can still tell yourself you're an honest person (even though you're not).

You are being deliberately vague when you

- talk and talk and talk about yourself without ever revealing any relevant information

- edit stories to give a false general impression that you were the victim instead of the victimizer

- try to conceal something by using words and phrases such as

    – "You might say . . ."

    – "Perhaps . . ."

    – "In a way . . ."

    – "Probably . . ."

    – "You could put it that way . . ."

    – "I suppose so . . ."

- avoid giving direct answers to direct questions

- use empty, nondisclosing phrases such as

    – "We talked about this and that . . ."

    – "You know what I'm saying . . ."

    – "If I feel like it . . ."

    – "It's going okay . . ."

    – "Someone told me . . ."

- say, "I'll think about it," when you're pinned down, though you never bring it up again. When you're challenged, you say, "I forgot"

TACTIC 3:

Staying Silent to Avoid Notice

Staying silent to avoid notice could also be called "trying to fly under the radar." Again, you try to avoid being challenged by "blending into the woodwork." You hope that if you keep your mouth shut, everyone will ignore you and you can cruise through life—and your treatment program—without putting in any effort.

The purpose of silence is to maintain your criminal and addictive lifestyle through secrecy. It is also a way to control others and to keep others at a distance. Sometimes you use silence to buy yourself time to size up another person so you can figure out how to manipulate him or her.

You use silence as a criminal tactic when you

- say, "I don't know and I don't care"
- refuse to listen or participate
- say, "I have no comment on that"
- say, "I just can't explain it" while shrugging or sighing
- say, "Nothing happened"
- say, "I don't have anything to say. They said it all"

TACTIC 4:

False Compliance

Like lying, *false compliance* shows up in two ways: compliance without commitment and passive resistance.

In your treatment program, *compliance without commitment* is an attempt to con the therapists into thinking that you're doing the work and making changes, while in fact you're just saying what you think they want to hear so they won't challenge you. You say the "right" things to staff, but you don't really mean what you say. You think that if you can keep the therapists happy, they won't notice that you're really just putting in time. You've also probably used compliance without commitment with your family, your spouse or partner, and an employer to get them off your case.

Passive resistance is a type of false compliance where you do the absolute minimum to get by. Not one little bit more. You don't actively fight the system, but you're determined not to give in to it by looking at your thinking and behavior and making changes.

Again, false compliance is an effort to look like you're doing what you're supposed to be doing, while in reality you are not doing the work. You appear to be agreeable to change, but you are really undermining opportunities for real change. In other words, you "talk the talk," but you don't "walk the walk." In the program, you learn all the right words and phrases—treatment talk—and use them like they mean something to you. But they don't. It's just another tactic you use to keep the spotlight off of you and your criminal and addictive thinking patterns.

You are using false compliance as a criminal tactic when you

- try to "score points" by saying the right thing or by doing the right thing just one time
- tell different people different versions of your thoughts and experiences depending on what you think they want to hear or what will make you look good in their eyes
- promise to change by saying, "I'll never do it again"
- claim to have changed by doing something right once
- try to convince therapists that you've completed treatment and learned everything you need to stay sober and crime free when in fact you're just restless, bored, and seeking excitement
- claim to have had a miraculous transformation
- say yes without meaning it

- fake interest with intense concentration, eye contact, and nodding head
- say, "I guess so," "You're right," or "It makes sense to me," when in fact you don't agree or it doesn't make sense to you or you simply don't care

TACTIC 5:

Playing Dumb

Playing dumb is an act you put on to try to convince others that you are too fragile, helpless, or stupid to be responsible so that they'll let you off the hook. Or you may tell staff you'd really like to look at those issues if only you had an idea of what they are talking about. Again, you try to fool others into thinking you're just not capable of making a responsible effort or don't understand what it is they are asking you to look at. You use this tactic to escape having to work at change.

You use playing dumb as a criminal tactic when you

- pretend to have less education or a lower reading ability than you really have in order to get out of making an effort
- frequently complain, "I didn't understand the question" or "I don't know what you are talking about" without making an effort to understand
- look blankly when you are confronted or challenged, as if you're incapable of understanding the situation and giving a meaningful response
- make simplistic or off-base comments in order to appear lost and confused
- exaggerate or make up mental or physical health problems to excuse your lack of compliance or effort
- complain about having too much to do or that the work is too hard

TACTIC 6:

Selective Memory and Attention

Selective memory and attention is yet another tactic for avoiding accountability. You remember only what's convenient to remember, so you won't be challenged or exposed. You also pay attention only to what you want to hear. You tune out anything that would make you uncomfortable about your criminal and addictive thinking and behavior.

You use selective memory and attention as a criminal tactic when you

- put off obligations by saying, "I forgot" or "I'm too busy right now" or "I'll do it later," even though you have little intention of ever following through

- ignore anything that challenges your thinking or lifestyle

- have little patience with ideas that don't fit in with yours

- believe the assignments and lectures in treatment don't apply to you—sometimes even before you've really looked at them

- twist statements that challenge your thinking around in your mind until you mistakenly believe they actually support your thinking

- pretend to listen by looking at the speaker and nodding or agreeing, while you are really thinking about other things that are more satisfying to you

- try to shift the responsibility for your lack of attention by claiming the speaker wasn't being clear

TACTIC 7:

Minimizing (Trivializing)

Minimizing, or trivializing, begins in your mind as a way to block out thoughts of your wrongdoing and deny the full extent of the harm you have caused others. Instead of denying what you did, you try to make it seem trivial or less significant than it is. You minimize when you

- play down the importance of a situation
- view your offenses as less serious than others do
- minimize the harm of your actions when you are held accountable
- claim you didn't *intend* to cause so much harm

Here are some examples of minimizing:

- "I just got into a little trouble."
- "It was a mistake—I was just playing a prank."
- "I caught a case" or "I found myself in a situation."
- "I only dealt a little crack. It's not like I used it."
- "I only did it a few times." (When in fact you've done it seven, eight, or more times, which would be "several" or "a lot," not "a few.")

■

You have probably used all of these avoidance tactics at one time or another. In fact, you probably are using many of them in your treatment program right now.

Minimizing, or trivializing, begins in your mind as a way to block out thoughts of your wrongdoing.

Identifying Your Avoidance Strategies

➤ Choose two tactics from the list of avoidance strategies on page 268 that you used *before* you were incarcerated this most recent time. Give a detailed example of how you used each tactic. Include what you hoped would happen when you used those tactics (how you hoped others would react, what you hoped to avoid, or what advantage you thought you'd gain).

EXAMPLE:

Avoidance tactic	How you used this tactic and what you hoped to gain by it
#2 Being deliberately vague	When I was out doing a job—burglaries or whatever—and my wife would ask where I'd been, I'd just say I'd picked up some day work with some guys. If she pushed for details, I'd get mad and accuse her of not trusting me. I wanted her to back off so she wouldn't find out I was doing crime again and get pissed off at me.

1. Avoidance tactic

_____

How you used this tactic and what you hoped to gain by it

_____

_____

_____

_____

2. Avoidance tactic

_____

How you used this tactic and what you hoped to gain by it

_____

_____

_____

_____

➤ Now write down two avoidance strategies you have used in treatment and give an example of how you've used each one. Explain what you hoped to get out of using that strategy each time.

1. Avoidance tactic

_____

How you used this tactic and what you hoped to gain by it

_____

_____

_____

_____

2. Avoidance tactic

_____

How you used this tactic and what you hoped to gain by it

_____

_____

_____

_____

Diversion Strategies

The second category of criminal and addictive tactics is _diversion strategies_. Again, diversion strategies are the tactics you use to confuse others, to misdirect attention away from yourself or from the most important issues, and to avoid exposure by keeping those around you off balance and distracted. You use diversion strategies for the same reasons you use all other tactics:

to help you continue an irresponsible way of thinking and living.

The seven basic tactics you use to divert attention from the work you need to do to change and the things you need to be accountable for are listed on the next page. (We've numbered them 8–14 to pick up where we left off with the avoidance strategies.)

8. pointing out the faults of others

9. magnifying (exaggerating significance)

10. deliberately trying to confuse

11. quibbling over words

12. introducing irrelevant issues

13. discussing smokescreen issues

14. using self-shaming to avoid responsibility

TACTIC 8:

Pointing Out the Faults of Others

One way you divert attention from your wrongdoings and from your criminal and addictive thinking is to *point out the faults and failures of others*. As long as you can keep the focus on someone else—"I'm not as bad as *he* is; *he's* the one who has got a lot of work to do"—you think you can get away with not taking responsibility for what you need to change. You point out the faults of your peers, your family, staff, administrators, the commissioner of corrections, the president of the United States—it doesn't matter who—because the purpose is to keep the focus on anyone other than you.

You are pointing out the faults of others as a criminal tactic when you

- make a big issue over a mistake made by staff

- get overly involved in giving critical feedback in group to peers in order to use up all the time and not allow the group an opportunity to give you critical feedback

- talk behind people's backs (backbiting) in order to get others focused on everyone else's shortcomings and issues and not yours

- criticize the appearance of others

TACTIC 9:

Magnifying (Exaggerating Significance)

Magnifying, or *exaggerating the significance,* of minor issues is a tactic you use to justify your behavior or divert attention from your own issues. Stirring up debate or conflict over small matters can also give you a sense of control and some easy thrills. You use this tactic just to see how far you can push somebody (giving you a feeling of power), to distract others, and to put others on the defensive. You take little things and blow them out of proportion.

You are using the magnifying criminal tactic as a diversion when you

- point out the small inconsistencies of others and then dwell on them

- try to start conflicts between peers or between staff and peers over minor issues

- keep the attention on others in the group by arguing with them about what they've shared, rather than just giving appropriate feedback

- go on and on about something good you've done or all the progress you've made in order to keep the focus off the work you still have to do

- play up the shortcomings of others while ignoring their genuine efforts at change

- exaggerate the fault of the other person in a conflict in order to make your role in the conflict seem less significant than it really is

TACTIC 10:

Deliberately Trying to Confuse

As a criminal and addictive thinker, you will sometimes *try to confuse* others in order to get the upper hand. Keeping others confused is a way of maintaining your sense of power and diverting attention from yourself and the important issues at hand. This tactic once again reveals how little respect you have for the truth. In fact, you use this tactic in part because you mistakenly believe the truth is your enemy.

You are deliberately trying to confuse others when you

- offer inconsistent versions of an event

- make serious points but, when challenged, say you were only joking

- jump around quickly from point to point

- speak so fast that others can't follow your words

- speak so slowly that others can't maintain interest in what you're saying

- use street language, personal slang, double-talk, or fancy words so that others won't be sure what you're really saying (in such cases, you are usually saying nothing)

- alter written material by changing dates or other key information

- misquote others by twisting the meaning of their words or claiming they said things they never said

- when challenged on a discrepancy or inconsistency, claim the listener misunderstood, thereby shifting the burden to the other person

- stop in the middle of a story, admit you were lying, and claim you're now going to tell the whole truth, when in fact you have no such intention

TACTIC 11:

Quibbling over Words

Quibbling over words is a way not only to divert attention from more important things but also to make yourself appear smart in front of peers or staff. By disputing the meaning of words or phrases someone else uses rather than trying to understand that person, you take control of the conversation by knocking it off track.

You are quibbling over words when you

- say, "I don't understand what you mean when you use that word that way"

- say, "What you say is incorrect—that phrase means [this] and not [that]"

- argue over the exact language used rather than trying to clarify the exact meaning intended

- misquote someone and then make a big deal claiming your version is correct

- if a staff member asks you if you know anything about the assault out on the yard, you say, "I didn't see the assault," even though you may know exactly who did it and why (you just didn't see the actual assault)

TACTIC 12:

Introducing Irrelevant Issues

Another tactic you use to divert attention away from yourself and your criminal and addictive behavior is *introducing irrelevant issues*. You may try to direct discussion toward things that interest you, such as cars, sports, politics, or music—anything to avoid discussing your crimes and your criminal and addictive thinking patterns. You may introduce your personal history—family troubles or social disadvantages growing up—to distract others from your recent behavior. Or you may introduce race, one of the most sensitive issues in this society and especially behind bars (as you know). As a criminal and an addict, you use race in order to justify, excuse, or keep the focus away from your behavior. And yes, race can be and is used as a diversion strategy by people of *all* races—including yours.

The fact is, your interests, your personal history, and race *are* important issues, and they deserve thought and discussion, but only in an appropriate way and time. Using them in any way to avoid looking at and changing your criminal and addictive thinking and behavior is introducing irrelevant issues. Like all the other tactics, its purpose is to allow you to keep thinking and living the way you have been—to avoid change.

You are introducing irrelevant issues when you

- use race to present yourself as a victim, thereby refusing to admit how you have been the victimizer

- charge racism when you don't get your own way or when your other tactics don't work and others continue to confront you

- constantly talk about your rights in order to avoid talking about your "wrongs"

- justify your crimes and alcohol and drug use with sad stories of how hard you've had it in life; even if the stories are true, they don't excuse your personal behavior and choices

- try to start arguments about other subjects when you are confronted by family, therapists, or peers

- blame your behavior choices on social injustice

TACTIC 13:

Discussing Smokescreen Issues

Smokescreen issues are slightly different from irrelevant issues. Smokescreen issues may be treatment issues that you use at inappropriate times in order to avoid disclosure. For example, you focus on some family issues in chemical dependency group or on your addiction in the family group.

Another form of using smokescreen issues is picking just one issue and keeping the discussion about your behavior as it relates to that issue at all times. If you have been diagnosed as depressed, you may talk about nothing else except your depression. It becomes a smokescreen issue when you use it to keep attention away from your criminal and addictive thinking and behavior. You say that if only you could take care of the depression, then you could really take advantage of the program and change. It's not that your depression is irrelevant to your thinking and behavior, it's that it is only one part of it.

You are using smokescreen issues when you

- keep writing the same Thinking Reports over and over

- discuss treatment issues in the wrong group or at the wrong time to keep from focusing on the subject at hand

- introduce physical or mental health problems just to excuse you from treatment work

TACTIC 14:

Using Self-Shaming to Avoid Responsibility

For those who prefer the diversion tactics, *using self-shaming to avoid responsibility* is often a last resort. When you are backed into a corner, you try to avoid taking a hard look at your behavior and thinking by shaming yourself publicly. You think that if you beat yourself up enough in front of peers and therapists, they'll let you off the hook. Or you may continually claim that your unresolved shame issues must be addressed before you can do the work at hand.

This diversion tactic should not be confused with your legitimate issues. The important difference between the two is the *reason* you are bringing up your feelings of shame. Are you just trying to distract attention or are you sincerely asking for help? Asking for help with shame issues is appropriate—at the right time and with the right person. Treatment, however, is not about shame. It's about *change*.

Self-shaming can be just another way to keep the attention of others off the fact that you still haven't done the work. Your self-shaming may be genuine or it may just be an act. It doesn't matter: Either way, you still haven't looked hard at your thinking and behavior and disclosed it to the group. You still haven't tried to make changes in how you think and live. You still haven't gotten honest.

You use self-shaming when you

- admit to and dwell on one crime or behavior to hide more serious ones

- talk and talk about what an awful person you are to get pity from others

Identifying Your Diversion Strategies

➤ Choose three tactics that you have used from the list of diversion strategies. Give a detailed example of how you used each tactic. Include what you hoped would happen when you used those tactics (how you hoped others would react, what you hoped to divert attention from, or what advantage you thought you'd gain).

EXAMPLE:

Diversion tactic	How you used this tactic and what you hoped to gain by it
#9 Magnifying (exaggerating significance)	When my cellmate took a pen from me without asking and I caught him using it working on one of the workbook exercises, I made a big deal about him disrespecting me and my property. But the thing is, I didn't really give a damn about the pen. I was just trying to rile things up and put it on him so I'd look good.

1. Diversion tactic

_____

How you used this tactic and what you hoped to gain by it

_____

_____

_____

_____

2. Diversion tactic

_____

How you used this tactic and what you hoped to gain by it

_____

_____

_____

_____

3. Diversion tactic

_____

How you used this tactic and what you hoped to gain by it

_____

_____

_____

_____

Aggression Strategies

To review, you use *aggression strategies* to attack, intimidate, and undermine the legitimate efforts of others. You actively try to create chaos through stirring up conflict, resentment, and other hard feelings. You take on the victim role, saying that others provoked you or at least didn't get out of your way. You tell yourself, then, that they are just getting what they deserve. You also try to make others fear you so they won't challenge your addictive and criminal thinking. Again, your main goals with aggression strategies are getting what you want, avoiding exposure and the zero state by keeping others on the defensive, and responding when you think you have been provoked or made to look bad.

The seven basic aggression strategies that criminals use to prevent others from confronting their thinking and behavior are listed below.

(We've numbered them 15–21 to pick up where we left off with the diversion strategies.)

15. arguing
16. using threatening words or behaviors (veiled or direct)
17. raging
18. sarcasm and teasing
19. splitting staff
20. creating chaos
21. attention seeking

TACTIC 15:

Arguing

Arguing is an aggressive criminal and addictive tactic you use to keep your distance from others and to get what you want. It is yet another strategy you have for protecting your criminal and addictive way of life.

Arguing turns a ***dialogue*** of ideas into just a war of words. Nobody learns anything new in an argument because arguing is not about learning, it's about winning. That means its only purpose is to pump up your ego and humiliate the other person.

You are using arguing as an aggressive criminal and addictive tactic when you

Dialogue

Dialogue is an exchange of ideas and opinions between two equals. The most important aspect of dialogue is that it is an *exchange.* That means ideas and opinions flow both ways and are taken in and considered by both people.

- raise your voice in a discussion, feel the adrenaline rush of battle, and focus only on proving the other person wrong

- refuse to listen to or think about what others are saying

- turn meanings around and attack (with words) the points of view of others

- try to turn the tables when you are confronted for not living up to an agreement by arguing that the other person misunderstood the agreement

- use anger and intensity to try to overpower others in a discussion and avoid having to look honestly at your deeper thoughts and fears

- turn conversations (dialogues) into power struggles and insist on having the last word

TACTIC 16:

Using Threatening Words or Behaviors (Veiled or Direct)

You use two types of *threatening words* and *behaviors* to try to control others, *veiled* and *direct*. Veiled threats are more hidden. They may include intimidating body language, such as threatening stares ("mean mugging") or flexing muscles in your arms and neck or clenching your fists. Veiled threats could also be vague statements that suggest "something bad" might happen to someone.

Direct threatening words and behaviors are more out in the open and include physical intimidation or statements of intent to cause harm. You use them to reinforce your feelings of superiority and entitlement and to avoid putdowns.

You are using veiled threatening words and behaviors when you

- say, "If I wasn't in this program trying to get healthy, you wouldn't be talking like that for long"

- say, "Where are the grievance forms?"

- say, "Remember what you did last weekend? It would be unfortunate if the staff found out"

- say, "My brothers ain't going to like that"

- use "mean mugging" or other threatening body language

You are using direct threatening words and behaviors when you

- hit or push someone

- say, "You're a dead man—my brothers will see to that"

- say, "Let's step into the bathroom where we can settle this like men"

- stand over someone flexing your muscles, staring, and making fists

- physically back someone down

- stalk others

- prey on the vulnerabilities of others

- curse at others

TACTIC 17:

Raging

You use *raging* as a tactic when you let yourself go wild with anger—yelling and screaming and threatening and throwing things (behavior guaranteed to put you in seg or get you thrown out of the program). You also use raging when you suggest that if someone doesn't leave you alone, you could explode at any time. You tell "war stories" about all the people you have beat up because you have a short fuse and can't control yourself. Raging is another way you attempt to control others—by making them keep their distance and making them afraid of you. You believe that someone who is afraid of you won't confront your criminal and addictive ways.

You are raging when you

- lose all control in anger and become wild and destructive

- make others believe you *could* lose all control and fly into a rage at any time, so they'd better treat you very carefully

Raging is another way you attempt to control others—by making them keep their distance and making them afraid of you.

TACTIC 18:

Sarcasm and Teasing

Sarcasm is sharp and mean-spirited language used to make others look stupid or worthless. You use it as an aggression tactic to build yourself up by putting others down. Sarcasm and *teasing* are strategies designed to control others by keeping them on the defensive. As with all aggression strategies, they are efforts to make you feel powerful and warn others to keep their distance.

You are using sarcasm and teasing when you

- are sharply critical and unforgiving when others slip up

- try to create an image of cool for yourself by making others appear foolish

- pick on others for their appearance or the way they talk

- try to embarrass, demean, or make fun of another with little digs or insults

- say, "I guess you wouldn't happen to know that . . ." in order to make someone look dumb

TACTIC 19:

Splitting Staff

Splitting staff is a common aggressive tactic used by people who are incarcerated and in treatment programs. Splitting staff is a variation of the old military strategy "divide and conquer." By trying to pit one staff member against another, you hope to decrease their authority and effectiveness and increase your influence and power. Lost in this game, of course, is any hope of your doing the treatment work and making the changes that could keep you out of prison and help you live responsibly in the world.

You are splitting staff when you

- tell one staff member, "You really understand me, unlike those other therapists"

- complain that staff members never explain things clearly, except for one or two particular therapists

- attack a staff member by saying, "You're the worst therapist here. All the others are better than you"

- twist stories around so one staff member will think that another is being unfair to you

- tell different versions of an incident to different staff members to try to put them in conflict

- go "staff shopping" until one finally gives you the answer you want

You may also use the splitting staff tactic to split your peer group. You are splitting peer groups when you

- say, "I can do treatment with him, but not with *that* guy"

- try to drum up support for yourself by "gathering a posse" while putting others down behind their backs

- try to purposely ruin someone's reputation by spreading rumors

TACTIC 20:

Creating Chaos

You are *creating chaos* as a tactic when you use a combination of other tactics to cause a constant disruption of programs, groups, exercises, and life on the unit. You may be spreading rumors (even about yourself) while you try to split staff, attack peers behind their backs, threaten peers in and out of group, accuse others of misunderstanding you, change your story depending on who is listening, argue over everything, and demand your rights. The idea is to keep the staff so busy dealing with the messes you make that the program grinds to a halt.

You create chaos in order to

- avoid working on your thinking and behavior and making changes

- get pleasure from the feeling of power and control it gives you

- feel like a big shot, that no treatment program is ever going to change *you*

TACTIC 21:

Attention Seeking

Attention seeking becomes an aggressive tactic anytime it disrupts the efforts of others to work the treatment program. Often you use bizarre or shocking behaviors or disclosures to stir things up.

You are using attention seeking as an aggressive criminal and addictive tactic when you

- threaten to quit the program

- do outrageous things to stand out and grab the group's attention or to intentionally upset people

- dress to show off a gang tattoo or muscles

- walk around like you are big, bad, and nationwide

- aggressively refuse to comply with staff

Identifying Your Aggression Strategies

➤ Choose two tactics that you have used from the list of aggression strategies. Give a detailed example of how you used each tactic. Include what you hoped would happen when you used those tactics (how you hoped others would react, what you hoped to divert attention from, or what advantage you thought you'd gain).

EXAMPLE:

Aggression tactic	How you used this tactic and what you hoped to gain by it
#18 Sarcasm and teasing	When X asked what "strategy" meant, I laughed out loud and said to the guy next to me, "They must not of gotten to that in the second grade," and I said it loud enough so several people around me could hear. I wanted to make X look like an idiot and make me look smart. I did it because it felt good to put him down. It also showed everybody I'm a hardass, so let me be.

1. Aggression tactic

_____

How you used this tactic and what you hoped to gain by it

_____

_____

_____

_____

2. Aggression tactic

_____

How you used this tactic and what you hoped to gain by it

_____

_____

_____

_____

Switching Strategies

As a criminal and addictive thinker, you have particular tactics you prefer. You may especially like aggression strategies because they seem to give you what you want most. Or you may be the type that thinks lying low—using avoidance strategies—is the most effective way of keeping people off your back and allowing you to continue your criminal and addictive lifestyle.

When your favorite tactics don't work, however, you will readily switch to another type to get what you want: power, control, and avoiding responsibility, accountability, and change. For example, some criminals and addicts who use avoidance strategies and appear passive will switch over immediately to aggressive, threatening tactics in a situation as soon as they figure out that the avoidance tactics aren't working. Understanding how you use all these tactics will help you begin to stop them and to find new behaviors that are more effective in getting along in the world.

Sometimes you may work your way "up the ladder," starting with avoidance, moving to diversion, and then getting aggressive. Sometimes you may use many strategies from all three groups in the space of just minutes! This is most likely to occur when you believe you aren't getting what you deserve, you are stressed out and feel cornered, or when you fear going into the zero state.

EXERCISE 86 EXERCISE

Identifying Your Pattern of Criminal and Addictive Tactics

▶ Which category of tactics—avoidance, diversion, or aggression strategies—do you use first?

_____

▶ Which tactics in that category are your favorites?

1. _____

   _____

2. _____

   _____

3. _____

   _____

➤ When that type of tactic doesn't work for you, which of the other two categories do you switch to first?

_____

➤ What are your favorite tactics in this second category?

1. _____

_____

2. _____

_____

3. _____

_____

➤ Are the tactics you used on the outside the same as what you tend to use on the inside? Why or why not?

_____

_____

_____

By understanding your use of criminal and addictive tactics and the thinking behind each of them, you can better understand and begin to change your criminal, irresponsible, and antisocial behavior. Now you are ready to start filling out the Tactics part on your Thinking Report on page 179.

Conclusion

Congratulations. By completing this workbook, you've learned that it is possible to change your thinking. This is good news. You now recognize that you have your own personal mental map that will give you direction and guide your behavior. Your personal mental map helps guide you through life.

This workbook has helped you learn how to think about your thinking. You've learned how to replace old patterns of thinking. A happier, healthier, more free way of life awaits you. And only you can make that happen.

Andrews, D. A., and James Bonta. *The Psychology of Criminal Conduct.* 2d ed. Cincinnati, Ohio: Anderson Publishing Co., 1998.

Beck, Aaron. *Prisoners of Hate: The Cognitive Basis of Anger, Hostility, and Violence.* New York: HarperCollins, 1999.

Beck, Aaron, Arthur Freeman, and Associates. *Cognitive Therapy of Personality Disorders.* New York: The Guilford Press, 1990.

Beck, Judith. *Cognitive Therapy: Basics and Beyond.* New York: The Guilford Press, 1995.

Burns, David D. *Feeling Good: The New Mood Therapy.* Revised. New York: Avon Books, Inc., 1999.

———. *The Feeling Good Handbook.* Revised. New York: Penguin Putman, Inc., 1999.

Greenberger, Dennis. *Mind Over Mood: Change How You Feel by Changing the Way You Think.* New York: The Guilford Press, 1995.

Jones, Dan. *Words for Our Feelings.* Austin, Tex.: Mandala, 1992.

Millon, Theodore, and Erik Siminsen, Morten Birket-Smith, Roger D. Davis, eds. *Psychopathy: Antisocial, Criminal, and Violent Behavior.* The Guilford Press: New York, 1998.

Nakken, Craig. *The Addictive Personality: Understanding the Addictive Process and Compulsive Behavior.* Center City, Minn.: Hazelden Publishing, 1996.

Samenow, Stanton E. *Inside the Criminal Mind.* New York: Times Books, 1984.

Twerski, Abraham J. *Addictive Thinking: Understanding Self-Deception.* 2d ed. Center City, Minn.: Hazelden Publishing, 1997.

Yochelson, Samuel, and Stanton E. Sameow. *The Criminal Personality: A Profile for Change.* Vol. 1. Northvale, N.J.: Jason Aronson, 1976.

———. *The Criminal Personality: The Change Process.* Vol. 2. Northvale, N.J.: Jason Aronson, 1977.

———. *The Criminal Personality: The Drug User.* Vol. 3. Northvale, N.J.: Jason Aronson, 1986.

REFERENCES

A NEW DIRECTION

A Cognitive-Behavioral Treatment Curriculum

Thinking Report

1. Event _____
   _____

2. Thoughts _____
   _____

3. Feelings _____
   _____

4. Behavior _____
   _____

5. Can you identify a core belief? _____
   _____

6. Alternative thoughts _____
   _____

7. Alternative behavior _____
   _____

Thinking distortions _____

Thinking patterns _____

Tactics _____

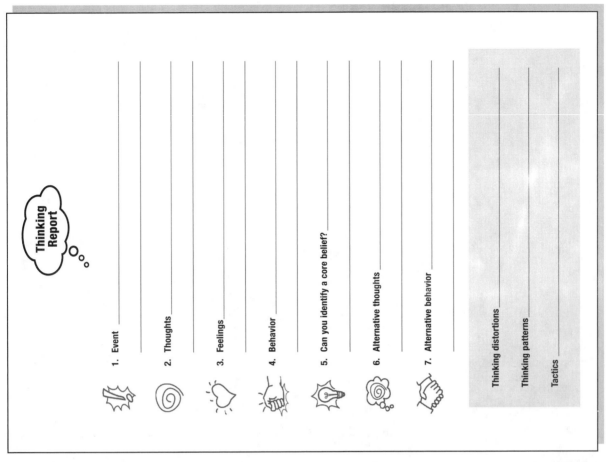

Thinking Report

1. Event _____

2. Thoughts _____

3. Feelings _____

4. Behavior _____

5. Can you identify a core belief? _____

6. Alternative thoughts _____

7. Alternative behavior _____

Thinking distortions _____

Thinking patterns _____

Tactics _____

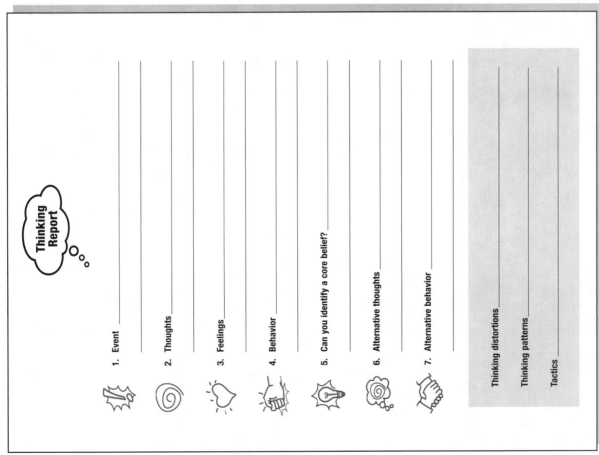

Thinking Report

1. Event _____

2. Thoughts _____

3. Feelings _____

4. Behavior _____

5. Can you identify a core belief? _____

6. Alternative thoughts _____

7. Alternative behavior _____

Thinking distortions _____

Thinking patterns _____

Tactics _____

NOTES

NOTES